LESS STRESS MORE SUCCESS

Accounting Revision

Higher Level

Michael McLoughlin

Gill & Macmillan

Gill & Macmillan

Hume Avenue

Park West

Dublin 12

with associated companies throughout the world

www.gillmacmillan.ie

© Michael McLoughlin 2011

978 0 7171 46994

Design by Liz White Designs

Print origination by MPS Limited, a Macmillan Company

*The paper used in this book is made from the wood pulp of managed forests.
For every tree felled, at least one tree is planted, thereby renewing natural resources.*

CONTENTS

3		80
3		80
1		60
2		100

Acknowledgments

Thanks to Rowena, Sean and Paul for all their help and patience. Thanks to Michael Freeley for all his advice and help. Thanks also to Aoileann O'Donnell of Gill & Macmillan who ensured that everything got finished.

Introduction

My main objective in devising this revision book for Leaving Certificate Accounting is to give students a good guide to the **practical application of the syllabus**. Accounting is a practical subject, and that means it must be **practised**. It is very little use reading through accounting questions – they must be attempted.

A famous sportsman once said: 'The more I practise, the luckier and better I get.' That applies with these questions too. The famous sportsman, incidentally, was golfer Gary Player, but his words must have been echoed by every successful sportsperson in history. That's how important practice is when it comes to delivering your best performance exactly when it's needed.

Get your timing right

In order to achieve a high grade in Leaving Certificate Accounting you must practise using relevant questions. That is what this book provides. But remember that **timing** is also very important.

There's no point in spending three-quarters of the exam on a question that only accounts for one-tenth of the marks. So you need to get used to the idea of dividing the available time sensibly to allow you to get the best possible mark Again, practice is the key.

The examination is three hours long. There are **400** marks in the exam. It is divided into three sections:

Section 1	
Do either:	
Question 1	120 marks
OR choose two out of:	
Questions 2, 3 and 4 @ 60 marks each	120 marks
(Tip – do Question 1 – only one topic to think about.)	
This translates into 30 per cent of the marks.	
30 per cent of the time = 54 minutes.	
Section 2	
Questions 5, 6 and 7 – do two of these @100 marks each.	200 marks
Each question is worth 25 per cent of the marks.	
25 per cent of the time = 45 minutes.	
(Tip – generally try to do Questions 6 and 7 even though Question 5 is always on ratios and analysis.)	
Section 3	
Questions 8 and 9 – do one of these @ 80 marks	80 marks
Each question is worth 20 per cent of the marks.	
20 per cent of the time = 36 minutes.	

What questions will come up?

Next, it's essential that you know the topics that are likely to appear in each of the three sections of the paper. Based on past papers, here are the topics you could be tested on in each question. Where you have a choice of questions to answer – for example in Section 1, where you can choose between answering Question 1 or answering two out of Questions 2, 3 and 4 – this should help you to plan in advance where your 'best' topics are likely to come up.

For a detailed look at which topics have come up in past years, see the table at the end of this introduction.

Section 1

Question 1. Final Accounts of one of:
- Company
- Sole trader
- Manufacturing
- Departmental

(Tip – they are all much the same.)

OR

Questions 2, 3 and 4. Two from:
- Farm Accounts
- Club Accounts
- Service Accounts
- Suspense Accounts
- Published Accounts
- Tabular Statements
- Cash Flow Statements
- Depreciation
- Revaluation
- Creditors Control
- Debtors Control

(Tip – a lottery! There's no way of knowing which of these the examiners will choose.)

Section 2

Two from:
- Ratios
- Incomplete Records
- Service Firms
- Club Accounts
- Suspense Accounts
- Published Accounts
- Farm Accounts
- Tabular Statements
- Cash Flow Statements

Section 3

Choose one from Questions 8 and 9:

Question 8. Costing
- Job and Product Costing
- Stock Valuation
- Marginal Costing

Question 9. Budgeting
- Production
- Cash
- Flexible

How to get the most out of your practice

As you practise more and more questions, you will start to speed up and be able to complete the work more quickly. Each time you complete a question, check your work using the supplied solutions.

In the beginning practise the **layout** of the questions and filling in all the figures. Try to do them quickly rather than neatly and do not add up the final figures. This is to help you build up your speed and confidence.

Later on, when you are more familiar with the method, do the questions more neatly, without using abbreviations and add up all the figures. This will get you into the habit of presenting your answers the way the examiners want to see them.

Devise your own personal revision timetable, giving more time to the areas that you consider yourself weaker in. The more often you get back to each area, the more successful you will be.

What the examiners are looking for

It is vital that you **show all your workings** as each partial element will gain some marks. This book's method means that you will not come to a full stop in any question, and remember: no one point or figure will count hugely. Here is what it says in the official marking schemes:

'Accounting solutions are mainly computational and most figures are made up of more than one component. **If a figure is wrong** per the solution, the **examiners** analyse the make-up of the candidate's figure and allocate marks for each correct **element included**.

Sometimes the solution to a part of a question may depend on the answer computed in another part of that question. Where their calculation in (a) is incorrect, but this inaccurate information is used in (b), examiners give credit for decisions correctly made on the basis of the incorrect data. **Candidates are not penalised twice for the same error.**'

They want you to succeed. By using the example questions in this book to plan your exam strategy and practice, practice, practice, you can give yourself the best chance of achieving that success.

exam focus

In this book, the solutions shown follow the official marking scheme for accounting in the Leaving Certificate Examinations.

The solutions are printed and the marks allocated to each line/figure are highlighted and shown in a circle like this **6** alongside. These marks are then totalled for each section/page and shown in a square like this **40**.

Table of past questions

Your guide to how often – and how recently – each topic has come up:

Topic	10	09	08	07	06	05	04	03	02	01	00	99	98
Section 1													
Company													
Sole Trader	Q1		Q1	Q1	Q1		Q1		Q1		Q1	Q1	Q1
Manufacturing		Q1				Q1		Q1		Q1			
OR													
Farm		Q4			Q2							Q3	Q2
Club			Q3										
Suspense									Q3				
Published			Q4		Q4			Q2					
Service						Q4							
Revaluation		Q3		Q3			Q3	Q4		Q3	Q3		Q4
Depreciation	Q3					Q3			Q2		Q2	Q2	
Tabular		Q2		Q4			Q2		Q4	Q2			
Cash Flow	Q2				Q3		Q4			Q4		Q4	
Creditors Control	Q4		Q2			Q2					Q4		Q3
Debtors Control				Q2				Q3					
Section 2													
Ratios								Q5 every year					
Published		Q6				Q6			Q6			Q6	

Years

Topic	10	09	08	07	06	05	04	03	02	01	00	99	98
Suspense	Q7		Q7		Q7		Q7				Q7		Q6
Service	Q6		Q6	Q6				Q6		Q6			
Cash Flow													Q7
Tabular					Q6							Q7	
Incomplete A				Q7		Q7					Q6		
B		Q7											
Club							Q6	Q7	Q7	Q7			
Section 3													
Marginal													
Costing	Q8	Q8	Q8	Q8	Q8	Q8	Q8	Q8	Q8	Q8	Q8	Q8	Q8
Budgeting													
Cash	Q9	Q9	Q9	Q9			Q9		Q9		Q9		
Production					Q9	Q9		Q9		Q9			
Flexible												Q9	Q9

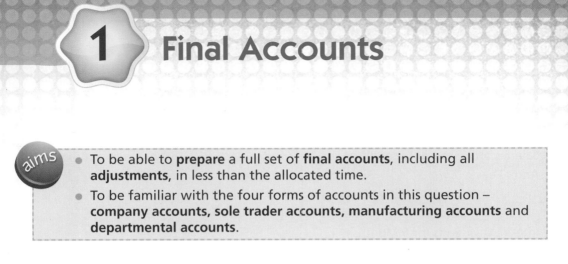

1 Final Accounts

aims
- To be able to **prepare** a full set of **final accounts**, including all **adjustments**, in less than the allocated time.
- To be familiar with the four forms of accounts in this question – **company accounts, sole trader accounts, manufacturing accounts** and **departmental accounts.**

Question 1 is always a set of final accounts. This question carries **120 marks**, which is **30 per cent** of the total. It is essential to practise these questions thoroughly.

The question involves a set of company, sole trader, manufacturing or departmental final accounts, each including a lot of adjustments.

key point

The fastest method is to lay out the questions in **blank form**. Enter the figures as they appear in the question beside the correct space in the blank form. Enter the figures in the first column and adjust them as required. The adjustments are included in the solutions to the questions.

exam focus

The basic rule is practise, practise, practise. Remember, if you are not going to answer question 1, then you must answer two questions from numbers 2, 3 and 4. Each of these questions carries 60 marks.

Question 1.1

Ballindine Ltd has an authorised share capital of €960,000 divided into 560,000 ordinary shares of €1 each and 400,000 11 per cent preference shares of €1 each. The following trial balance was extracted from its books at 31 December 2010:

Entry	Debit (€)	Credit (€)
Issued Capital: Ordinary Shares		450,000
Preference Shares		200,000
Profit and Loss		18,000
Stocks (Including Heating Oil €1,500)	48,500	
Debtors and Creditors	55,400	63,200
Buildings at Cost	495,000	
Delivery Vans (Cost €160,000)	105,000	
12% Debentures		125,000

Provision for Bad Debts		2,000
Bank		34,000
Light and Heat	5,000	
Purchases and Sales	590,000	830,000
9% Investments (1/1/2010)	150,000	
Salaries and General Expenditure	86,700	
Audit Fees	14,000	
Insurance of Vans (Including Suspense)	5,800	
Advertising (Incorporating 4 Months' Investment Income)	18,000	
Interim Dividends for 6 Months	28,000	
Debenture Interest Paid for First 4 Months	5,500	
Directors' Fees	35,300	
Goodwill	80,000	
	1,722,200	1,722,200

You are also given the following information:

1. Stock at 31 December 2010 was valued at €52,300. This includes heating oil of €900 and stocks that cost €4,000 and have a net realisable value of €2,500.

2. The suspense figure arises because an incorrect figure was entered for debenture interest (although the correct figure has been entered in the bank account) and purchases returns of €800 were entered only in the creditors account.

3. Goods sent to a customer on approval on 31 December 2010 had been entered in error as a credit sale. The selling price of these goods was €4,500, which represents cost plus 50 per cent mark-up.

4. Repairs to delivery vans costing €3,000 were carried out by the firm's own workforce. €500 of this represented parts taken from the firm's own stocks, and the remainder represented salary paid.

5. Provide for depreciation at the rate of 20 per cent of cost per annum from date of purchase to date of sale. On 31 July 2010 a van that had cost €15,000 on 1 April 2007 was traded against a new van costing €20,000. An allowance of €6,000 was received for the old van.

   The cheque for the net amount was treated in error as a purchase of trading stock, and this was the only entry made in the books.

6. The directors recommend:
   (a) The preference dividend due be paid.
   (b) A final dividend of 10 per cent be paid on the ordinary shares.
   (c) Provision be made for debenture interest due.
   (d) A bad debt of €400 be written off and the provision for bad debts be adjusted to 4 per cent of the remaining debtors.

You are required to prepare:

(a) Trading and profit and loss accounts for the year ended 31 December 2010.

(b) Balance sheet at 31 December 2010.

Solution to Question 1.1

Ballindine Ltd

(a) Trading and Profit and Loss Accounts for the Year Ended 31 December 2010

	Workings	(€)	(€)	(€)
Sales		825,500		
Less Costs				
Opening Stock		47,000		
Purchases		574,700		
		621,700		
Closing Stock		52,900		
			568,800	
Gross Profit			256,700	
Investment Income	W5		13,500	
Profit on Disposal			1,000	
				271,200
Less Expenses				
Establishment and Administration				
Light and Heat	W2	5,600		
Salaries and General		84,200		
Directors' Fees		35,300		
			125,100	
Financial				
Audit Fees		14,000		
Bad Debt		400		
Increase in Provision		20		
Selling and Distribution			14,420	
Van Insurance	W3	7,100		
Delivery Van Repairs		3,000		
Depreciation for Year		32,417		
Advertising	W4	22,500	65,017	204,537
Operating Profit				66,633
Less interest	W6			15,000
Net Profit				51,633

Less Appropriations				
Ordinary Dividend		Paid	17,000	
		Proposed	45,000	(62,000)
Preference Dividend		Paid	11,000	
		Proposed	11,000	(22,000)
				(32,337)
Add P & L Balance 1/1/2010				18,000
P & L Balance 31/12/2010				(14,337)

(b) Balance Sheet at 31 December 2010

	Workings	Cost (€)	Depreciation (€)	Net Book Value (€)
Fixed Assets				
Buildings		495,000		495,000
Vans	W1	165,000	77,417	87,583
		660,000	77,417	582,583
9% Investment				150,000
Goodwill				80,000
				812,583
Current Assets				
Stock			52,900	
Debtors		50,500		
Less Provision for Bad Debts		(2,020)	48,480	
Stock of Heating Oil	W2		900	
Investment Income Due	W5		9,000	
			111,280	
Current Liabilities				
Creditors		63,200		
Bank		34,000		
Debenture Interest Due	W6	10,000		
Ordinary Dividend Due		45,000		
Preference Dividend Due		11,000		
Working Capital/Net Current Assets			163,200	(51,920)
				760,663
Financed by		Authorised	Issued	
OSC		560,000	450,000	
11% Preference Shares		400,000	200,000	
		960,000		650,000

Reserves	
Profit and Loss	(14,337)
Long-Term Liabilities	
12% Debentures	125,000
	760,663

Workings

W1

	Cost (€)	Depreciation (€)	Net Book Value (€)
Vans	160,000	(55,000)	105,000
	(15,000)	10,000	(5,000)
	20,000		

Depreciation on Old Van

2004 $15,000 \times 20\% \times \frac{3}{4} =$	2,250
2005–2006 $15,000 \times 20\% \times 2 =$	6,000
2007 $15,000 \times 20\% \times \frac{7}{12} =$	1,750
	10,000

Depreciation for Year

$145,000 \times 20\% =$	29,000
$15,000 \times 20\% \times \frac{7}{12} =$	1,750
$20,000 \times 20\% \times \frac{5}{12} =$	1,667
	32,417

W2

Light and Heat

(€)			(€)
1,500	Profit & Loss		5,600
5,000	Balance		900
6,500			6,500
Balance 900			

W4

Advertising

	(€)		(€)
	18,000	Profit & Loss	22,500
Investment	4,500		
	22,500		22,500

W3

Van Insurance (Including Suspense)

(€)			(€)
5,800	Profit & Loss		7,100
500			
800			
7,100			7,100

W5

Investment Income

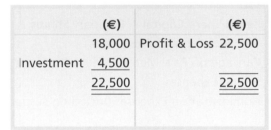

	(€)		(€)
Profit & Loss	13,500	Advertising	4,500
		Balance	9,000
	13,500		13,500
Balance	9,000		

Question 1.2

James Ltd, a manufacturing firm, has an authorised capital of €800,000 divided into 50,000 ordinary shares at €1 each and 250,000 eight per cent preference shares at €1 each. The following trial balance was extracted from its books at 31 December 2010:

	(€)	(€)
Factory Buildings (Cost €450,000)	405,000	
Plant and Machinery (Cost €260,000)	156,000	
Discount (Net)		4,000
Profit and Loss Balance 1/1/2010		82,300
Stocks on Hand 1/1/2010		
Finished Goods	85,500	
Raw Materials	48,000	
Work in Progress	24,150	
Sales		935,000
General Factory Overheads	50,300	
Patents	70,000	
Purchase of Raw Materials	450,280	
Sale of Scrap Materials		5,500
Hire of Special Equipment	12,000	
Debtors and Creditors	94,400	57,700
Interim Dividends (6 Months)	17,000	
Bank		11,450
Direct Factory Wages	198,220	
9% Debentures (Including €30,000 Issued on 1/4/2010)	100,000	
VAT		12,730
Issued Share Capital – Ordinary Shares		300,000
– Preference Shares		200,000
Carriage on Raw Materials		5,510
Selling Expenses		68,420
Administration Expenses (Including Suspense)	23,900	
	1,708,680	1,708,680

The following information and instructions are to be taken into account:

1. Stocks on hand at 31/12/2010:

	(€)
Finished goods	92,000
Raw materials	51,000
Work in progress	28,550

The figure for finished goods includes items which cost €7,000 to produce, but now have a sales value of €4,500.

2. Included in the figure for sale of scrap materials is €1,800 received from the sale of an old machine on 30/6/2010. This machine had cost €22,000 on 1/4/2006. The cheque had been entered in the bank account. This was the only entry made in the books.

3. The suspense figure arises as a result of discount allowed €1,000 entered only in the debtors account.

4. It was discovered that finished goods, which cost €8,000 to produce, were invoiced to a customer on a 'sale or return' basis. These goods had been entered in the books as a credit sale at cost plus 20 per cent.

5. During 2010 James Ltd built an extension to the factory. The work was carried out by the company's own employees. The cost of their labour, €40,000, was included in factory wages. The cost of materials used, €18,000, is included in purchases. No entry was made in the books in respect of this extension.

6. Depreciation is provided on fixed assets as follows:
   Plant and machinery – 20% of cost per annum from date of purchase to date of sale.
   Factory buildings – 2% of cost at 31/12/2010.

7. The directors are proposing that:
   (a) The preference dividend due be paid.
   (b) The total ordinary dividend for the year should be 9c per share.
   (c) Provision should be made for debenture interest.
   (d) Corporation tax of €10,000 be provided for.

8. Goods should be transferred from factory at current market value €800,000.

You are required to prepare:

(a) Manufacturing, trading and profit and loss account for the year ended 31/12/2010. **75**

(b) Balance sheet as at 31/12/2010. **45**

Solution to Question 1.2 **35**

(a) Manufacturing Account of James Ltd for the Year Ended 31/12/2010

	Workings	€	€
Opening Stock of Raw Materials			48,000 ❶
Purchases of Raw Materials	W1		432,280 ❸
Carriage In			5,510 ❷
			485,790
Less Closing Stock of Raw Materials			51,000 ❶
Cost of Raw Materials Consumed			434,790

Direct Costs:			
Factory Wages	W2	158,220 ❹	
Hire of Special Equipment		12,000 ❷	170,220
Prime Costs		**605,010**	
Factory Overheads:			
General Factory Overheads		50,300 ❷	
Depreciation on Plant and Machinery	W3	49,800 ❸	
Depreciation on Buildings		10,160 ❸	
Loss on Sale of Machine	W4	1,500 ❹	
Factory Cost			111,760
			716,770
Work in Progress 1/1/2010			24,150 ❷
			740,920
Less Work in Progress 31/12/2010			(28,550) ❷
			712,370
Less Sale of Scrap Materials	W5		(3,700) ❹
Cost of Manufacture			708,670 ❶
Gross Profit on Manufacture			91,330
Goods Transferred from Factory at CMV			800,000 ❶

Trading and Profit and Loss Account for Year Ended 31/12/2010   40

	Workings	€	€
Sales	W6		925,400 ❺
Opening Stock of Finished Goods		85,500 ❷	
Goods Transferred @ CMV		800,000 ❷	
		885,500	
Less Closing Stock of Finished Goods	W7	97,500 ❻	
Cost of Goods Sold		788,000	(788,000)
Gross Profit on Trading			137,400
Gross Profit on Manufacture			91,330
			228,730
Less Expenses:			
Administration Expenses			
Administration Expenses	W8	22,900 ❻	

Selling and Distribution Expenses:

Selling Expenses		68,420 ❷	(91,320)
			137,410
Discount (Net)	W9		3,000 ❸
Operating Profit			140,410
Less Debenture Interest	W10		(8,325) ❹
Net Profit before Taxation			132,085
Less Taxation			(10,000) ❷
Profit after Tax			122,085
Less Preference Dividend Paid		8,000 ❶	
Preference Dividend Due		8,000 ❶	
Ordinary Dividend Paid		9,000 ❶	
Ordinary Dividend Due		18,000 ❶	
			(43,000)
Retained Profit			79,085
Profit and Loss Balance 1/1/2010			82,300 ❷
Profit and Loss Balance 31/12/2010			161,385 ❷

(b) Balance Sheet of James Ltd as at 31/12/2010 `45`

Intangible Assets

Patents					70,000 ❷

Tangible Assets:	Workings	Accumulated Cost €	Depreciation €	Net €	
Factory Buildings	W11	508,000 ❷	55,160 ❷	452,840	
Plant and Machinery	W3,12	238,000 ❷	135,100 ❸	102,900	
		746,000	190,260	555,740	555,740
					625,740
Current Assets:					
Stocks Raw Materials			51,000 ❷		
Work in Progress			28,550 ❷		
Finished Goods			97,500 ❷	177,050	
Debtors	W13			84,800 ❺	
				261,850	

Creditors: Amounts Falling Due within One Year:

Trade Creditors	57,700 ❷	
Bank	11,450 ❷	
VAT	12,730 ❷	
Dividends Due	26,000 ❹	
Taxation	10,000 ❷	
Debenture Interest Due	8,325 ❸	126,205
Net Current Assets		135,645
		761,385

Financed By:
Creditors: Amounts Falling Due after More than One Year

9% Debentures			100,000 ❷

Capital and Reserves:	**Authorised**	**Issued**	
Ordinary Shares at €1 Each	550,000 ❶	300,000 ❷	
8% Preference Shares at €1 Each	250,000 ❶	200,000 ❷	
	800,000	500,000	
Profit and Loss Balance 31/12/2010		161,385	
			661,385
			761,385

Workings

1. Purchases of Raw Materials	450,280 − 18,000 = 432,280	
2. Factory Wages	198,220 − 40,000 = 158,220	
3. Depreciation on Plant and Machinery	26,000 + 23,800 = 49,800	
	47,600 + 2,200 = 49,800	
Accumulated Depreciation on Plant	104,000 − 18,700 + 49,800 = 135,100	
4. Loss on Disposal of Machine	22,000 − 18,700 − 1,800 = (1,500)	
5. Sale of Scrap Materials	5,500 − 1,800 = 3,700	
6. Sales	935,000 − 9,600 = 925,400	
7. Closing Stock of Finished Goods	92,000 − 2,500 + 8,000 = 97,500	
8. Administration Expenses	23,900 − 1,000 = 22,900	
9. Discount	4,000 − 1,000 = 3,000	
10. Debenture Interest	6,300 + 2,025 = 8,325	
Debenture Interest	1,575 + 6,750 = 8,325	
11. Cost of Factory Buildings	450,000 + 18,000 + 40,000 = 508,000	
12. Cost of Plant and Machinery	260,000 − 22,000 = 238,000	
13. Debtors	94,400 − 9,600 = 84,800	

Question 1.3

Carey Ltd has an authorised capital of €990,000, divided into 690,000 ordinary shares at €1 each and 300,000 seven per cent preference shares at €1 each. The following trial balance was extracted from its books on 31/12/2010:

	€	€
Land and Buildings at Cost	780,000	
Accumulated Depreciation – Land and Buildings		39,000
Patents (Incorporating 2 Months' Investment Income Received)	58,200	
6% Investments 1/5/2010	180,000	
Delivery Vans at Cost	172,000	
Accumulated Depreciation – Delivery Vans		78,000
Stocks 1/1/2010	76,600	
Purchases and Sales	620,000	990,000
Directors' Fees	80,000	
Salaries and General Expenses	176,000	
Debenture Interest Paid	4,500	
Profit and Loss Balance 1/1/2010		67,600
Debtors and Creditors	73,900	81,000
Provision for Bad Debts		3,600
Interim Dividends for First 6 Months	40,000	
9% Debentures (Including 780,000 9% Debentures Issued at Par on 31/3/2010)		230,000
VAT		16,500
Bank		5,500
Issued Capital		
550,000 Ordinary Shares at €1 Each		550,000
200,000 7% Preference Shares €1 Each		200,000
	2,261,200	2,261,200

The following information and instructions are to be taken into account:

1. Stock at 31/12/2010 at cost was €85,000 – this figure includes old stock which cost €8,000 but has a net realisable value of 60 per cent of cost.

2. Patents which incorporated two months' investment income are to be written off over a five-year period commencing in 2010.

3. Provide for depreciation on delivery vans at the annual rate of 20 per cent of cost from the date of purchase to the date of sale.

   Note: On 31/9/2010 a delivery van which had cost €60,000 on 1/6/2008 was traded in against a new van which cost €84,000. An allowance of €22,000 was given on the old van. The cheque for the net amount of this transaction was incorrectly treated as a purchase of trading stock. This was the only entry made in the books in respect of this transaction.

4. Buildings are to be depreciated at the rate of two per cent of cost per annum (land at cost was €130,000). At the end of 2010 the company revalued the land and buildings at €880,000.

5. The figure for bank in the trial balance has been taken from the firm's bank account. However, a bank statement dated 31/12/2010 has arrived showing a credit balance of €4,040. A comparison of the bank account and the bank statement has revealed the following discrepancies:

(a) Investment income €2,700 had been paid direct to the firm's bank account.

(b) A cheque for €780, issued to a supplier, had been entered in the books (cash book and ledger) as €870.

(c) A credit transfer of €750 had been paid direct to the firm's bank account on behalf of a debtor who had recently been declared bankrupt. This represents a first and final payment of 30c in the €1.

(d) A cheque for fees of €6,000 issued to a director had not yet been presented for payment.

6. The directors recommend that:

(a) The preference dividend due be paid.

(b) A final dividend on ordinary shares be provided, bringing the total dividend up to 9c per share.

(c) Provision be made for both investment income and debenture interest due.

(d) Provision for bad debts be adjusted to four per cent of debtors.

You are required to prepare:

(a) Trading and profit and loss account for the year ended 31/12/2010.   75

(b) Balance sheet as at 31/12/2010.   45

120 marks

Solution to Question 1.3   75

(a) Trading, Profit and Loss Account for the Year Ended 31/12/2010

	Workings	€	€	€
Sales				990,000 ❷
Less Cost of Sales				
Stock 1/1/2010			76,600 ❷	
Add Purchases	W1		558,000 ❺	
			634,600	
Less Stock 31/12/2010	W2		(81,800) ❺	(552,800)
Gross Profit				437,200

Less Expenses				
Administration				
Directors' Fees		80,000 ❷		
Salaries and General Expenses		176,000 ❷		
Patents Written Off	W3	12,000 ❻		
Depreciation – Buildings	W4	13,000 ❹	281,000	
Selling and Distribution				
Bad Debts Written Off		1,750 ❹		
Depreciation – Delivery Vans	W5	35,600 ❻		
Loss on Sale of Van	W7	10,000 ❺	47,350	328,350
Operating Profit				108,850
Decrease in Provision for Bad Debts	W6		744 ❺	
Investment Income	W8		7,200 ❹	7,944
				116,794
Debenture Interest				(18,900) ❺
Net Profit for Year before Taxation				97,894
Less Appropriation				
Preference Dividend Paid			7,000 ❷	
Ordinary Dividend Paid			33,000 ❸	
Preference Dividend Proposed			7,000 ❷	
Ordinary Dividend Proposed			16,500 ❸	(63,500)
Retained Profit				34,394
Profit and Loss Balance 1/1/2010				67,600 ❷
Profit and Loss Balance 31/12/2010				101,994 ❻

(b) Balance Sheet at 31 December 2010 `45`

	Workings	Cost €	Accumulated Depreciation €	Net €	Total €
Intangible Fixed Assets					
Patents (60,000 – 12,000)					48,000 ❸
Tangible Fixed Assets					
Land and Buildings	W9	880,000 ❶		880,000	
Delivery Vans	W10	196,000 ❷	85,600 ❸	110,400	
		1,076,000	85,600	990,400	990,400
Financial Assets					
8% Investments					180,000 ❷
					1,218,400

Current Assets

Stock			81,800 ❷	
Investment Income Due			2,700 ❸	
Debtors	W11	71,400 ❸		
Less Provision		2,856 ❶	68,544	
			153,044	

Creditors: Amounts Falling Due within One Year

Creditors	W12	81,090 ❸		
Preference Dividend Due		7,000 ❷		
Ordinary Dividend Due		16,500 ❸		
Debenture Interest Due		14,400 ❸		
VAT		16,500 ❷		
Bank	W13	1,960 ❺	(137,450)	
				15,594
				1,233,994

Financed by

Creditors: Amounts Falling Due after More than One Year

8% Debentures			230,000 ❷

Capital and Reserves	Authorised	Issued	
Ordinary Shares at €1 Each	690,000	550,000 ❶	
6% Preference Shares at €1 Each	300,000	200,000 ❶	
	990,000	750,000	
Revaluation Reserve W14		152,000 ❸	
Profit and Loss Balance		101,994	
Shareholders' Funds			1,003,994
Capital Employed			1,233,994

Workings

1. Purchases	620,000 − 62,000 = 558,000
2. Closing Stock	85,000 − 3,200 = 81,800
3. Patents Written Off	(€58,200 + €1,800) × 20% = 12,000
4. Depreciation − Buildings	2% of (780,000 − 130,000) = 13,000
5. Depreciation − Delivery Vans	25,800 + 9,800 = 35,600
	34,400 + 1,200 = 35,600
	22,400 + 9,000 + 4,200 = 35,600
6. Decrease in Provision for Bad Debts	3,600 − 2,856 = 744
7. Loss on Sale of Van	60,000 − 22,000 − 28,000 = 10,000
8. Investment Income	1,800 + 2,700 + 2,700 = 7,200
9. Land and Buildings at Cost	780,000 + 100,000 = 880,000

10. Delivery Vans at Cost	172,000 + 84,000 − 60,000 = 196,000
Accumulated Depreciation D. Vans	78,000 + 35,600 − 28,000 = 85,600
11. Debtors	73,900 − 750 − 1,750 = 71,400
12. Creditors	81,000 + 90 = 81,090
13. Bank Overdraft as per Trial Balance	5,500
Less Investment Income	(2,700)
Less Credit Transfer Received	(750)
Less Bank under Credited	(90) = (1,960)
Alternative	(4,040 − 6,000) = (1,960)
14. Revaluation Reserve	100,000 + 39,000 + 13,000 = 152,000

Question 1.4

The following trial balance was extracted from the books of M. O'Brien on 31/12/2010:

	€	€
9% Investments 1/6/2010	200,000	
Buildings (Cost €980,000)	933,000	
Delivery Vans (Cost €150,000)	80,500	
5% Fixed Mortgage (Including Increase of €200,000		
5% Mortgage Received on 1/4/2010)		500,000
Patents (Incorporating 3 Months' Investment Income)	55,500	
Debtors and Creditors	77,600	86,500
Purchases and Sales	668,000	982,000
Stocks 1/1/2010	67,700	
Commission	24,000	
Provision for Bad Debts		3,800
Salaries and General Expenses	194,100	
Discount (Net)		4,600
Rent		15,000
Mortgage Interest Paid for First 3 Months	4,000	
Insurance (Incorporating Suspense)	8,700	
VAT		5,500
PRSI		2,300
Bank		70,900
Drawings	37,500	
Capital		680,000
	2,350,600	2,350,600

The following information and instructions are to be taken into account:

1. Stock at 31/12/2010 at cost was €74,500. This figure includes damaged stock which cost €6,600 but which now has a net realisable value of €1,900.

2. Provide for depreciation on vans at the annual rate of 15 per cent of cost from the date of purchase to the date of sale.

   Note: On 31/3/2010 a delivery van which had cost €42,000 on 31/5/2007 was traded against a new van which cost €48,000. An allowance of €20,000 was made on the old van. The cheque for the net amount of this transaction was entered in the bank account but was incorrectly treated as a purchase of trading stock. These were the only entries made in the books in respect of this transaction.

3. Patents, which incorporate three months' investment income, are to be written off over a five-year period commencing in 2010.

4. The suspense figure arises as a result of the posting of an incorrect figure for mortgage interest to the mortgage interest account and discount received of €700, entered only in the creditors account. The correct interest was entered in the bank account.

5. Provision to be made for mortgage interest due.

6. A new warehouse was purchased during the year for €240,000 plus VAT of 12.5 per cent. The amount paid to the vendor was entered in the buildings account. No entry was made in the VAT account.

7. Provide for depreciation on buildings at the rate of two per cent of cost per annum. It was decided to revalue the buildings at €1,100,000 on 31/12/2010.

8. Provision for bad debts to be adjusted to four per cent of debtors.

You are required to prepare:

(a) Trading and profit and loss account for the year ended 31/12/2010. `75`

(b) Balance sheet as at 31/12/2010. `45`

`120 marks`

Solution to Question 1.4   `75`

(a) Trading, Profit and Loss Account for the Year Ended 31/12/2010

	Workings	€	€	€
Sales				982,000 ❷
Less Cost of Sales				
Stock 1/1/2010			67,700 ❷	
Add Purchases	W1		640,000 ❻	
			707,700	
Less Stock 31/12/2010	W2		(69,800) ❻	(637,900)
Gross Profit				344,100

Less **Expenses**

Administration

Salaries and General Expenses		194,100 ❷	
Patents Written Off	W3	12,000 ❻	
Insurance	W4	9,650 ❽	
Depreciation – Buildings	W5	19,000 ❸	234,750

Selling and Distribution

Loss on Sale of Delivery Van	W7	4,150 ❻		
Commission		24,000 ❷		
Depreciation – Delivery Vans	W6	23,175 ❺	51,325	(286,075)
				58,025

Add Operating Income			
Reduction in Provision for Bad Debts	W8		696 ❹
Rent			15,000 ❷
Discount	W9		5,300 ❺
Operating Profit			79,021
Investment Income			10,500 ❸
			89,521
Mortgage Interest	W10		(22,500) ❻
Net Profit for Year			67,021 ❼

(b) Balance Sheet as at 31 December 2010   `45`

	Workings	Cost €	Accumulated Depreciation €	Net €	Total €
Intangible Fixed Assets					
Patents (€60,000 – €12,000)					48,000 ❹
Tangible Fixed Assets					
Buildings	W11	1,100,000 ❷		1,100,000	
Delivery Vans		156,000 ❷	74,825 ❸	81,175	
		1,256,000	74,825	1,181,175	1,181,175
Financial Assets					
Investments					200,000 ❷
					1,429,175
Current Assets					
Stock				69,800 ❷	
VAT	W12			24,500 ❺	
Investment Income Due				6,000 ❸	
Debtors			77,600 ❷		
Less Provision			3,104 ❶	74,496	
				174,796	

Creditors: Amounts Falling Due within One Year

Creditors	86,500 ❷		
Mortgage Interest Due	18,750 ❸		
PRSI	2,300 ❷		
Bank	70,900 ❷	(178,450)	(3,654)
			1,425,521

Financed by:

Creditors: Amounts Falling Due after More than One Year

9% Fixed Mortgage		500,000 ❷

Capital and Reserves

Capital 1/1/2010		680,000 ❶	
Add Net Profit		67,021 ❶	
		747,021	
Less Drawings		37,500 ❷	
		709,521	
Revaluation Reserve	W13	216,000 ❹	925,521
Capital Employed			1,425,521

Workings

1. **Purchases**		668,000	
Less Payment for Van		(28,000)	640,000
2. **Closing Stock**		74,500	
Less Valueless Stock		(4,700)	69,800
3. **Patents**			
(€55,500 + €4,500) ÷ 5			12,000
4. **Insurance**		8,700	
Add Mortgage Interest		250	
Add Discount Received		700	9,650
5. **Depreciation – Buildings**			
2% of €950,000			19,000
6. **Depreciation – Delivery Vans**			
(€22,500 + €675) or (€5,625 + €17,550) or (€16,200 + €1,575 + €5,400)			23,175
7. **Loss on Sale of Van**			
(€42,000 − €17,850 − €20,000)			4,150 loss
Provision for Depreciation – Vans			
(€69,500 − €17,850 + €23,175)			74,825
8. **Provision for Bad Debts**			
(€3,800 − €3,104)			696 CR

9. **Discount**	4,600	
Add Unrecorded Discount	700	5,300
10. **Mortgage Interest**	4,000	
Less Suspense	(250)	
Add Interest Due	18,750	22,500
11. **Buildings**	98,000	
Less VAT	(30,000)	
Add Revaluation	150,000	1,100,000
12. **Vat Account**	5,500	
Less VAT on Buildings	(30,000)	24,500
13. **Revaluation Reserve**		
Land and Buildings	150,000	
Provision for Depreciation (47,000 + 19,000)	66,000	216,000

Question 1.5

The firm of Donnelly Limited is divided into two departments – Footwear and Sportswear. The following balances were extracted from its books on 31/12/2010:

	€	€
Authorised and Issued Share Capital		
Ordinary Shares at €1 each		400,000
7% Preference Shares at €1 each		300,000
Buildings (Cost €800,000)	740,000	
Fittings and Equipment at Cost	160,000	
Accumulated Depreciation: Fittings and Equipment		38,400
Debtors and Creditors	73,000	56,000
9% Debentures (Including €40,000 9%		
Debentures Issued on 30/06/2010)		140,000
Footwear Department		
Stock 1/1/2010	42,000	
Purchases and Sales	390,000	600,000
Carriage Inwards	6,000	
Sportswear Department		
Stock 1/1/2010	27,000	
Purchases and Sales	270,000	400,000
Returns Outwards		3,000
Interim Dividends for First 6 Months	30,000	
Profit and Loss 1/1/2010	15,000	
Salaries and General Expenses	75,400	

Directors' Fees	24,000	
Debenture Interest Paid for First 6 Months	6,300	
Advertising Account 1/1/2010		1,500
Advertising	12,000	
VAT	4,800	
PAYE/PRSI		2,300
Light and Heat		11,200
Provision for Bad Debts		2,100
Bank		96,600
	1,983,300	1,983,000

You are given the following additional information:

1. Stocks at 31/12/2010: Footwear €45,000, Sportswear €32,000.

2. Sportswear which cost €6,000 was sent to a customer on a sale or return basis in December. These goods were incorrectly treated as a credit sale at a mark-up on cost of 50 per cent.

3. During the year new fittings were installed in the shop. The materials were included in error in Sportswear purchases. These materials had cost €7,000 and the labour costing €4,000 was provided by the employees.

4. Depreciation is to be provided as follows:

   Buildings: two per cent of cost

   Fittings and Equipment: 20 per cent of book value.

   At the end of the year the company revalued the buildings at €960,000.

5. The payment for advertising was for a two-year advertising campaign which commenced on 1/10/2009.

6. The floor space of the firm is divided as follows: Footwear 75 per cent, Sportswear 25 per cent.

7. Expenses applicable to both departments should be divided on the basis of sales or floor space where appropriate.

8. The directors recommend:
   (a) The payment of the balance of the debenture interest.
   (b) The payment of the balance of the preference dividend.
   (c) The payment of a final dividend on the ordinary shares to bring the total dividend for the year up to 10%.
   (d) To provide for taxation of €60,000.

You are required to:
(a) Prepare departmental trading and profit and loss account for the year ending 31/12/2010.

(**b**) Prepare balance sheet at 31/12/2010.

(**c**) Explain why is it advisable for firms to prepare departmental accounts.

Solution to Question 1.5

(a) Departmental Trading, Profit and Loss Account for the Year Ending 31/12/2010

	Workings		Footwear	Sportswear	Total
Sales	W1		600,000	391,000	991,000
Less Cost of Sales					
Opening Stock			42,000	27,000	69,000
Purchases			390,000	263,000	653,000
Carriage			6,000	—	6,000
Returns Outwards			—	(3,000)	(3,000)
			438,000	287,000	725,000
Less Closing Stock			(45,000)	(38,000)	(83,000)
Cost of Sales			393,000	249,000	642,000
Gross Profit			207,000	142,000	349,000
Less Expenses	Basis				
Distribution					
Advertising	T.O.	W6	3,600	2,400	6,000
Salaries	T.O.		42,840	28,560	71,400
Depn. Fitts & Eq	F.S.		19,890	6,630	26,520
	66,330		7,590	103,920	
Administration					
Light and Heat	F.S.		8,400	2,800	11,200
Directors' Fees	T.O.		14,400	9,600	24,000
Depn. Buildings	F.S.		12,000	4,000	16,000
			34,800	16,400	51,200
Total Expenses			101,130	53,990	155,120
Operating Profit			105,870	88,010	193,880
Interest	F.S.		10,800	3,600	14,400
			95,070	84,410	179,480
Taxation					60,000
					119,480
Dividends:	Paid			30,000	
Proposed			31,000	61,000	
Retained Profit					58,480
Balance 1/1/2010		W5			15,000
Balance 31/12/2010					43,480

(b) Balance Sheet at 31/12/2010

Fixed Assets	Workings	Cost	Acc. Depn	Net
Buildings	W2	960,000	—	960,000
Fittings and Equipment	W3	171,000	64,920	106,080
		1,131,000	64,920	1,066,080
Current Assets				
Stock Footwear		45,000		
Sportswear	W7	38,000	83,000	
Debtors		64,000		
Less Provision		2,100	61,900	
Advertising Prepaid	W6		4,500	
VAT		4,800		
Bank		69,600		
		250,800		
Less Current Liabilities				
Creditors		56,000		
PAYE/PRSI		2,300		
Interest		8,100		
Dividends	W4	31,000		
Taxation		60,000	157,400	
Net Current Assets				93,400
				1,159,480
Financed by				
9% Debentures		180,000		
Authorised and Issued Share Capital				
€1 Ordinary Shares		400,000		
7% €1 Preference Shares		300,000	700,000	
Reserves				
Profit and Loss				43,480
Revaluation		236,000	279,480	1,159,480

Workings

1. Total Preference Dividend = 300,000 × 7% = 21,000
   Total Ordinary Dividend = 400,000 × 10% = 40,000

	Ord.	Pref.	Total	
Paid	19,500	10,500	30,000	
Proposed	20,500	10,500		31,000
Total	40,000	21,000		61,000
2. Buildings	800,000	(60,000)	740,000	
Depreciation		(16,000)	(16,000)	
Revaluation	160,000	76,000	236,000	
	960,000	—	960,000	
3. Fittings & Equipment		160,000	(38,400)	121,600
		Purchases Spw.	7,000	
Salaries	4,000			
132,600 × 20% Depreciation		(26,520)		
	171,000	(64,920)	106,080	

4. Debenture Interest = 140,000 × 9% × $^6/_{12}$ = 6,300

   = 180,000 × 9% × $^6/_{12}$ = 8,100

   = 14,400

5. Profit and Loss Balance is a Loss Carried Forward.

6.

		Advertising		
	T/b	12,000	T/b	1,500
		P/L	6,000	
		Bal	4,500	

7. Sales Sportswear 400,000 − 9,000 = 391,000
   Debtors 73,000 − 9,000 = 64,000
   Closing Stock Sportswear 32,000 + 6,000 = 38,000

(c) Why prepare departmental accounts?

So that management will know the sales, cost of sales, gross profit, operating expenses and net profit or loss of each department.

This information will enable them to make better decisions about the running of the business. This may involve closing unprofitable departments, relocating departments, giving more/less space to different departments, allocating more/fewer staff to different departments.

2 Ratios and Analysis

Ratios

These are the ratios you'll need to know:

key point

It is essential that all the ratios are known. Even more important is the ability to comment on the significance of the ratios.

1. Gross Profit Percentage/Margin = Gross Profit/Sales × 100/1

2. Mark-Up Percentage = Gross Profit/Cost of Sales × 100/1

3. Rate of Stock Turnover = Cost of Sales/Average Stock

4. Net Profit Percentage/Margin = (Net Profit/Sales) × 100/1

5. Length of Credit Given to Debtors = (Trade Debtors/Credit Sales) × 365 (Days)

6. Length of Credit Received from Creditors = (Trade Creditors/Credit Purchases) × 365 (Days)

7. Interest Cover = Profit before Interest & Tax/Interest

8. Working Capital Ratio = Current Assets/Current Liabilities (Ideal 2/1)

9. Liquid Asset Ratio = Liquid Assets/Current Liabilities (Acid Test Ratio) **NB** (Ideal 1/1)

10. Capital Gearing Ratio = (Debentures + Preference Shares)/Capital Employed × 100/1

11. Return on Capital Employed **NB** = Operating Profit/Capital Employed × 100/1 (Should be above the return on risk-free investment)

12. Return to Equity Shareholders Profit after Interest, Tax & Preference Dividend/Shareholders' Equity × 100/1

13. Earnings per Share = Profit after Interest, Tax & Preference Dividend/No. of Ordinary Shares (**Answer in cents**)

14. Price Earnings Ratio = Market Price per Share/Earnings per Share

15. Dividend per Share = Ordinary Dividend/No. of Ordinary Shares (**Answer in cents**)

16. Dividend Cover = Net Profit/Ordinary Dividend

17. Dividend Yield = (Dividend per Share/Market Price) × 100/1

Indicators of bankruptcy

The indicators of bankruptcy have been developed in the US and are called **'Z scores'**. The higher the score, the less likelihood of insolvency. The results show that almost every company that failed in a particular year showed warning signs in the previous year's results.

Practise writing out the ratios until you are absolutely sure that you know them all.

Five ratios are used:

1. $\dfrac{\text{Working Capital}}{\text{Total Assets}}$
2. $\dfrac{\text{Retained Earnings}}{\text{Total Assets}}$
3. $\dfrac{\text{Profit before Interest and Tax}}{\text{Total Assets}}$
4. $\dfrac{\text{Market Value}}{\text{Total Assets}}$
5. $\dfrac{\text{Sales}}{\text{Total Assets}}$

When you are asked for a particular ratio, do not just write down the answer. Write down the **formula in words**. Then write down the first line of the **formula in figures**. Finally, show all your calculations to the last line. For example,

Issued Ordinary Share @ €1 €500,000

10% Preference Shares @ €1 €300,000

Net Profit €150,000

(ignore tax)

You are asked for the earnings per share

$$\text{Earnings per Share} = \frac{\text{Net Profit} - \text{Preference Dividend} - \text{Tax}}{\text{Number of Ordinary Shares}}$$

$$= \frac{150,000 - 30,000}{500,000}$$

$$= \frac{120,000}{500,000} = 24 \text{ cent}$$

(Note: The cent designation is essential.)

When asked to **comment** on the performance of the company – whether the company is a good investment either on the part of a prospective shareholder or of a lending institution – it is vital that you are able to comment properly and make proper comparisons.

The following are the key areas.

1. Profitability

Profitability – return on capital employed and return to equity shareholder; compare to present return on risk-free investment. Compare with previous year if possible.

2. Liquidity

Current ratio 1.5 to 2 : 1.
Quick ratio 1 : 1.

3. Gearing

A lowly geared company cannot get into financial difficulty. High gearing **may** be acceptable if the company is highly profitable.

4. Trends

If you are given figures for only one year, it is very difficult to do anything other than look at the reserve figures. If you are given results for more than one year, there are a lot of comparisons that can be made, and it is a matter of emphasising the most important.

5. Company Sector

Comment and compare to industry norm if given.

6. Company Name

Look at company title to see if it is a plc or a private company.

7. Fixed Assets

Look for full breakdown, giving composition and depreciation policy.

8. Debentures

Rate of interest and amount of interest and interest cover. Refer back to gearing, look at redemption date and effect on future liquidity.

9. Dividends

Dividend cover and yield are important to ensure that dividends are not paid out of reserves. Look at the market price of the shares. If the company is not a plc, note that there is not a ready market for the shares.

10. Purchase of Shares

If being asked to buy shares in the company, see if the number of shares being bought would give control of the company. Look at the cost of borrowing and the present dividend policy.

11. Loan

If being asked to lend to the company, state that you must know for what purpose the finance is required and how the future interest cover, capital gearing ratio and liquid asset ratio will be affected.

12. Investments

If the company has investments, compare cost and market value to see if selling these might help alleviate any liquidity problem the company might have.

13. Earnings

Look at earnings per share and price earnings ratio, and consider the industry norm if one is given.

14. Audit

State that in order to comment fully on a particular company, you would require a full set of unqualified audited accounts for a number of years.

If the company has liquidity/profitability problems and you are asked to suggest some type of corrective action, you might suggest some of the following: sale and leaseback, factoring of debtors, sale of investment, issue of shares (if possible), capital reduction scheme or even closedown.

Question 2.1

The following are the summarised final accounts of two manufacturing companies, Soda Ltd and Tonic Ltd, for the year ended 31 December 2010.

Summarised Profit and Loss Accounts for the Year Ended 31 December 2010

	Soda Ltd		Tonic Ltd	
	(€)	(€)	(€)	(€)
Sales		700		540
Cost of Goods Sold		310		230
Gross Profit		390		310
Debenture Interest	40		20	
Other Expenses	190	230	140	160
Net Profit		160		150

Balance Sheet at 31 December 2010

	(€)	(€)	(€)	(€)
Fixed Assets at Cost		820		370
Accumulated Depreciation		360		80
		460		290
Current Assets				
Trade Debtors	115		60	
Stocks	80		40	
Bank	10			
	205		100	
Current Liabilities				
Trade Creditors	80		55	
Net Current Assets		125		45
		585		335
Financed by				
Shareholders' Funds		345		220
Debentures		240		115
		585		335

The following information is also available:

1. Approximately 90 per cent of each company's sales are made on credit.
2. Each company's stock level remains approximately constant throughout the year.

Requirement:

Write a report to the managing director of Soda Ltd comparing the performance of her company with that of Tonic Ltd. Your report should include reference to appropriate ratios and any other information that you consider relevant.

Solution to Question 2.1

Your answer should be put into report format with comments on the following:

	Soda Ltd	Tonic Ltd
Gross Profit (%)	55.71	57.41
Net Profit (%)	22.86	27.78
Return on Capital Employed	34.19	50.75
Expenses/Sales (%)	32.86	29.63
Interest Cover	5	8.5
Working Capital Ratio	2.56 : 1	1.82 : 1
Liquid Asset Ratio	1.56 : 1	1.09 : 1
Credit to Debtors (days)	66	45
Credit from Creditors (days)	94	87
Stock Turnover	3.88	5.75
Working Capital/Total Assets	0.19	0.12
Debt/Equity	0.7 : 1	0.52 : 1

Question 2.2

The following figures have been taken from the final accounts of Gill plc, a wholesaler in home computers and games software, whose authorised capital is €1,000,000, made up of 800,000 ordinary shares at €1 each and 100,000 eight per cent preference shares at €2 each. The firm has already issued 500,000 ordinary shares and 50,000 preference shares.

	(€)
Fixed Assets (Cost €500,000)	490,000
Investments (Market Value €80,000)	160,000
Current Assets (Stock €200,000, Debtors €69,000)	269,000
Current Liabilities (Bank €2,000, Trade Creditors €90,000)	92,000
General Reserve (1/1/2010)	25,000
9% Debentures 2012 Secured	90,000
Sales	920,000
Opening Stock	58,000
Cost of Sales	730,000
Total Expenses for the Year	96,000
Profit and Loss Balance (1/1/2010)	18,000 CR
Profit and Loss Balance (31/12/2010)	12,000 CR
Proposed Dividends	32,000

(a) Calculate the following:

    (i) Dividend per ordinary share.

    (ii) Interest cover.

    (iii) Market value of one ordinary share whose dividend yield is five per cent.

    (iv) Cash sales if the average period of credit is 1.2 months.

    (v) Price earnings ratio.

(b) Would the shareholders be satisfied with the policies, performance and state of affairs of the above company? Use relevant ratios and information to support your answer.

(c) Comment on the liquidity of Gill plc and suggest appropriate action.

Solution to Question 2.2

(a)

(i) Dividend per Ordinary Share

$$\frac{\text{Ordinary Dividend}}{\text{Number of Ordinary Shares}} = \frac{24,000}{500,00} = 4.8 \text{ cent}$$

(ii) Interest Cover

$$\frac{\text{Net Profit} + \text{Interest}}{\text{Interest}} = \frac{94,000 + 8,100}{8,100} = 12.6 \text{ times}$$

(iii) Market Value of One Ordinary Share

$$\frac{\text{Dividend per Share} \times 100}{\text{Market Price}} = \frac{4.8 \times 100}{5 \times \text{Market Price}} = 96 \text{ cent}$$

(iv) Cash Sales

$$\frac{69,000 \times 12}{\text{Credit Sales}} = 1.2$$

Credit Sales = 690,000

Total Sales = 920,000

Cash Sales = 920,000 − 690,000 = €230,000

(v) Price Earnings Ratio

$$\frac{\text{Market Price}}{\text{Earnings per Share}} = \frac{96}{18.8} = 5.1 : 1$$

(b)

Trends: Gill plc has increased its reserves from €43,000 at the beginning of the year to €105,000 at the end of the year. This has more than doubled its reserves even after providing for dividends amounting to €32,000. This would seem to suggest an improved performance over recent years.

Profitability: The firm's profitability is satisfactory. The return on capital employed and the returns to equity shareholders of 12.8 and 15.9 per cent, respectively, are better than the return available at present from risk-free investments. The earnings per share is 18.8 cent, and it would take 5.6 years for a share to recoup its market price.

Dividend policies: The dividends are covered 2.9 times. Therefore the shareholders are receiving 34 per cent of available profits. The policy of paying out dividends is creating cash flow problems for the company. The dividend per share is 4.8 cent and the dividend yield is five per cent, whereas the preference shareholders receive eight per cent.

Investment policy: The investments have dropped 50 per cent in value, from €160,000 to €80,000. This places a question mark over its investment policy.

Debentures: The debentures are due for repayment in 2009. This will put a great strain on the firm's liquidity. As the debentures are secured on the fixed assets, the repayments could place the future of Gill plc in jeopardy, as the two per cent depreciation indicates that these assets are buildings or they are totally under-depreciated, and therefore the depreciation policy must be questioned.

Sector: Gill plc is involved in the home computer and games software business. This is a very competitive sector.

Closing stock: The shareholders would be very concerned that the firm's huge closing stock is more than four times its opening stock.

Interest cover: The interest cover is 12.6 times. This is a very favourable situation and indicates that borrowings are being put to good use.

Gearing: The firm is low-geared as the fixed-interest capital is 24 per cent of total capital employed.

The shareholders would not be satisfied with the policies and state of affairs but would be satisfied with the performance of Gill plc.

(c)

The working capital ratio and acid test ratio are 2.2 : 1 and 0.6 : 1, respectively. The working capital ratio is above the accepted norm of 2 : 1. This shows that working capital is sufficient to meet the day-to-day costs of running the firm. The firm should not let this go too high above 2 : 1, as this would indicate a build-up of stock or a poor use of resources.

The acid test ratio is below the accepted norm of 1 : 1. This shows more accurately the ability of the firm to pay its short-term debts. Gill plc would have difficulty paying its immediate debts:

1. Sell investments. Any surplus cash not required for working capital should be reinvested more profitably. Income from this would improve profitability.

2. Sell stock at an auction and raise at least €55,000.

3. Make a rights issue of about 60,000 shares.

4. Sell some of the fixed assets and lease back.

5. Delay the payments of dividends.

Question 2.3

The balance sheets of J. Giles are as follows:

	31 March 2009		31 March 2010	
	(€)	(€)	(€)	(€)
Fixed Assets		260,000		205,000
Current Assets				
Stocks	86,000		84,000	
Debtors	94,000		58,000	
	180,000		142,000	
Current Liabilities	(174,000)	6,000	(59,000)	83,000
		266,000		288,000
Capital				
Opening Balance	262,900			266,000
Add Net Profit	15,600			36,000
Less Drawings	(12,500)			(14,000)
Closing Balance	266,000			288,000

The following information was extracted from the trading accounts for the years ended 31 March 2009 and 2010, respectively.

	2009 (€)	2010 (€)
Sales	505,000	385,000
Gross Profit	152,900	172,750
Opening Stock	82,000	86,000

Required:

Calculate the following ratios for each year and comment on the position shown for the second year as compared with the first:

(a) Gross profit ratio.

(b) Stock turnover.

(c) Working capital ratio.

(d) Acid test ratio.

(e) Period of credit given.

Solution to Question 2.3

(a) Gross Profit Ratio

= (Gross Profit × 100)/Sales

Year Ended 31 March 2009: €152,900 × 100/€505,000 = 30.3%

Year Ended 31 March 2010: €172,750 × 100/€385,000 = 44.9%

The ratios have increased from 30.3 to 44.9 per cent. Possible explanations are:

(i) Changes in the types of goods sold, where some lines carry different rates of gross profit than others.

(ii) Increase in the selling price of goods without a proportionate increase in the cost price.

(iii) Elimination of inefficiencies and factors such as theft which would reduce the profit margin.

(b) Stock Turnover

= Cost of Sales/Average Stock

where Cost of Sales = Sales Gross Profit.

Year Ended 31 March 2009: €352,100/€84,000 = 4.2 times

Year Ended 31 March 2010: €212,250/€85,000 = 2.5 times

In the first year the average stock was turned over 4.2 times. This has deteriorated to 2.5 times in the second year. This has happened because although sales and purchases have fallen considerably, stock levels have remained relatively constant. It may well be possible to reduce stock levels if this reduction is likely to be permanent.

(c) Working Capital Ratio

= Current Assets : Current Liabilities

As at 31 March 2009: €180,000 : €174,000 = 1.04 : 1

As at 31 March 2010: €142,000 : €59,000 = 2.41 : 1

Current assets were roughly equal to current liabilities at 31 March 2009. However, Mr Giles might have difficulty paying his liabilities on time, depending on how quickly his current assets could be turned into cash. His position at 31 March 2010 appears comfortable, with current assets equal to 2.41 times current liabilities.

(d) Acid Test Ratio

= Current Assets – Stock : Current Liabilities

As at 31 March 2009: €94,000 : €174,000 = 0.54 : 1

As at 31 March 2010: €58,000 : €59,000 = 0.98 : 1

At 31 March 2009, quick assets (those readily convertible into cash) amounted to only 54 per cent of current liabilities. If the current liabilities are required to be paid promptly, Mr Giles would not be able to meet these in full. At 31 March 2010, quick assets approximately equalled current liabilities, and he should then have been in a position to meet the total liabilities.

(e) Period of Credit Given

= (Debtors × 365)/Sales

Year Ended 31 March 2009: (€94,000 × 365)/€505,000 = 68 days

Year Ended 31 March 2010: (€58,000 × 365)/€385,000 = 55 days

The average period of credit given to customers has decreased from 68 days to 55 days. This ratio reflects the time taken by customers to pay and should approximate the credit terms allowed by the business. The situation has improved and, viewed in conjunction with the fall in sales, this would suggest that Mr Giles has been more selective in deciding to whom he sells goods on credit.

Question 2.4

The following figures have been extracted from the final accounts of O'Gara Plc, a manufacturer in the healthcare industry, for the year ended 31 December 2010.

Trading and Profit and Loss Account for Year Ended 31/12/2010

	€
Sales	980,000
Cost of Goods Sold	(620,000)
Total Operating Expenses for Year	(207,000)
Interest for Year	(10,000)
Net Profit for Year	143,000
Proposed Dividends	(68,000)
Retained Profit for Year	75,000

Ratios and Figures for Year Ended 31/12/2009

Earnings per Ordinary Share	18c
Dividend per Ordinary Share	6.5c
Quick Ratio	0.75 to 1
Market Price of Ordinary Share	€1.90
Return on Capital Employed	14%
Return on Equity Funds	7.6%
Interest Cover	9 times
Gearing	35%

Balance Sheet as at 31/12/2010

Intangible Assets	160,000	
Tangible Assets	790,000	950,000
Current Assets (including stock €66,000, debtors €74,000)		160,000
Trade Creditors		(73,000)
Dividends		(68,000)
		969,000
10% Debentures 2010/2011		100,000
Issued Capital		
650,000 Ordinary Shares @ €1 Each		650,000
100,000 13% Preference Shares @ €1 Each		100,000
Profit and Loss Balance		119,000
		969,000

You are required to:
(a) Calculate the following for 2008:
>   (i) Cash sales if the average period of credit to debtors is one month.
>   (ii) Earnings per share.
>   (iii) The market price of one ordinary share if the price earnings ratio is 11.
>   (iv) The ordinary dividend cover.
>   (v) The dividend yield. **50**

(b) A friend of yours has been given the opportunity to buy ordinary shares in O'Gara Plc but before doing so asks your opinion. What advice would you give? Use ratios, percentages and other information from the above to support your conclusions. **50**

100 marks

Solution to Question 2.4

(a) **50**

(i) **Cash Sales**

$$\frac{\text{Debtors} \times 12}{\text{Credit Sales}} = 1 \qquad \text{Credit Sales} = \frac{74,000 \times 12}{1}$$

Credit Sales = 888,000

Cash Sales = 980,000 − 888,000 = **€92,000** ⑫

(ii) **Earnings per Share**

$$\frac{\text{Net Profit} - \text{Pref Div} \times 100}{\text{Number of Ordinary Shares}} = \frac{130,000 \times 100}{650,000} = \textbf{20c} \; ⑩$$

(iii) Market Price

$$\frac{\text{Market Price}}{\text{Earnings per Share}} = 11$$

$$\frac{x}{20} = 11 \qquad = \qquad \textbf{220c} \ \text{⑧}$$

(iv) Dividend Cover

$$\frac{\text{Net Profit after Pref Div}}{\text{Ordinary Dividend}} = \frac{130,000}{55,000} \qquad = \textbf{2.4 times} \ \text{⑩}$$

(v) Dividend Yield

$$\frac{\text{Dividend per Share} \times 100}{\text{Market Price}} = \frac{8.46c \times 100}{220c} \qquad = \qquad \textbf{3.85\%} \ \text{⑩}$$

(b) I would advise my friend to buy shares in O'Gara Plc for the following reasons: **50**

Gearing ⑩
Gearing is 20.6 per cent or 0.26 : 1. The company is low-geared at 20.6 per cent and interest cover is 15.3 times. Therefore there is little risk from outside investors. Last year's gearing and interest cover were 35 per cent and nine times, respectively. These figures indicate improved situations and that the company is less at risk and is better able to pay interest in 2010 than in 2009. The prospects of being able to pay dividends are good.

Dividends ⑩
Dividend per share is 8.46c. The dividend per share has increased from 6.5c since 2009. The company's dividend cover is 2.4 times and dividend yield is 3.85 per cent. The dividend policy is such that a shareholder can expect a decent amount of profits will be paid out each year, while at the same time the long-term prospects of capital gain are good. The real return to ordinary shareholders would be 9.1 per cent based on available profits.

Profitability ⑩
O'Gara Plc is a profitable firm because its return on capital employed of 15.8 per cent and on equity funds of 6.9 per cent indicate that the firm is earning much more (three times) than the return from risk-free investments of about four per cent to six per cent. These are big increases from 14 per cent and 7.6 per cent, respectively, in 2009. The earnings per share has increased by 2c from 18c in 2009 to 20c in 2010.

Liquidity ⑩
O'Gara Plc has a liquidity problem. It would have difficulty paying its immediate debts. This difficulty has worsened since 2009 and the company is less able to pay its immediate debts in 2010, as indicated by the acid test ratio. This ratio has worsened from 0.75 in 2009 to 0.67 in 2010. This ratio indicates that O'Gara Plc has only 67c available to pay each €1 owed immediately. The company had 75c available in 2009.

Reserves ❺
The firm is retaining profits and building up reserves, which augurs well in the long term and should bring about an increase in the market price of the share. Reserves have risen by €75,000 to €119,000 since 2007.

Market price ❺
The share value has gone up by 30c to €2.20 since 2009 and is likely to continue in its upward movement based on current-year performance.

Real value of fixed assets/security
The real value of fixed assets and intangible assets should be questioned. There are no write-offs. Although there are intangible assets valued at €160,000 there is little risk to the company, as this is only 20 per cent of the tangible fixed assets and this ensures that there is adequate security for the loan.

Sector
The healthcare industry is a growth area and the sector has good prospects.

Price earnings ratio
The price earnings ratio is 11. This means that at the present rate of earnings it would take 11 years to earn back the price of a share.

Interest cover
Interest cover is 15.3 times and has improved from nine times in 2009. There should be more profits available to the shareholders.

Question 2.5

The following figures have been extracted from the final accounts of Coulter Ltd, a service provider in the leisure industry, whose authorised capital is €900,000, made up of 650,000 ordinary shares at €1 each and 250,000 10 per cent preference shares.

Trading and Profit and Loss Accounts for Year Ended 31/12/2010

		€
Sales		1,100,000
Costs of Goods Sold		
Stock 1/1/2010	63,000	
Purchases	751,000	
Stock 31/12/2009	(74,000)	(740,000)
Total Operating Expenses for the Year		(208,000)
Interest for Year		(15,000)
Net Profit for Year		137,000
Proposed Dividends		(66,000)
Retained Profits for Year		71,000

Ratios and Figures for Year Ended 31/12/2009

Earnings per Ordinary Share	22c
Dividend per Ordinary Share	2.9c
Quick Ratio	0.9 to 1
Market Value of Ordinary Share	€1.75
Return on Capital Employed	14%
Return on Equity Funds	19%
Interest Cover	9 times
Gearing	40%

Balance Sheet as at 31/12/2010

Intangible Assets	140,000	
Fixed Assets	760,000	900,000
Current Assets	170,000	
Current Liabilities		
Trade Creditors	(35,000)	
Proposed Dividends	(66,000)	69,000
		969,000
9% Debentures 2015/2016		160,000
Issued Capital		
500,000 Ordinary Shares @ €1 Each	500,000	
200,000 10% Preference Shares @ €1 Each	200,000	
Profit and Loss Balance	109,000	809,000
		969,000

You are required to answer the following:

(a) (i) Cash purchases if the average period of credit received from creditors is
1.5 months.

(ii) Earnings per share.

(iii) How long it would take one ordinary share to recoup (recover) its 2009 market
price based on present dividend payout rate.

(iv) The dividend yield for 2009.

(v) The market value of one ordinary share in 2010 if the price earnings ratio is 9.

50

(b) Assume that the company wishes to raise further finance by issuing the remaining
shares at €2 per share. Would you as a shareholder be prepared to purchase these
shares? Outline your reasons for purchasing/not purchasing some shares. Your
answer should include all relevant information included in the above figures and
references to any other information that you consider necessary.

50

100 marks

Solution to Question 2.5

(a) **50**

(i) **Cash Purchases**

$$\frac{\text{Creditors} \times 12}{\text{Credit Purchases}} = 1.5 \text{ Credit Purchases} = \frac{35,000 \times 12}{1.5}$$

Credit Purchases $= 280,000$

Cash Purchases $= 751,000 - 280,000 = €471,000$ ⑫

(ii) Earnings per Share

$$\frac{\text{Net Profit after Div} \times 100}{\text{Number of Ordinary Shares}} = \frac{117,000 \times 100}{500,000} = 23.4c \ \text{⑩}$$

(iii) Period to Recover Price

$$\frac{\text{Market Price}}{\text{Dividend per Share}} = \frac{175}{9.2} = 19 \text{ years} \ \text{⑫}$$

(iv) Dividend Yield

$$\frac{\text{Dividend per Ordinary Share} \times 100}{\text{Market Price}} = \frac{2.9 \times 100}{1.75} = 1.66\% \ \text{⑧}$$

(v) Price Earnings Ratio

$$\frac{\text{Market Price}}{\text{Earning per Share}} = 9 = \frac{\text{Market Price}}{23.4} = 9 \ 210.6c \ \text{⑧}$$

(b)   **50**

Dividends ⑩

	2010	2009
Dividend per Share	92c	2.9c
Dividend Yield	4.37%	1.66%
Dividend Cover in 2008	2.5 times	7.6 times
Real Return − Div Yield × Div Cover	10.9%	12.6%

The dividend policy of the company has eased over the two years as the percentage of profits paid out has increased from 13.15 per cent to 40 per cent.
The real returns of 10.9 per cent and 12.6 per cent are well above the return from risk-free investments of less than five per cent.

Market value of shares ⑧
The market value of each share increased from €1.75 in 2009 to €2.11 in 2010. The shares are now being offered at €2.00. This is 11c above the 2010 value. The price earnings ratio in 2010 is 9 (8 in 2009).

Profitability ⑧
The return on shareholders' equity increased from 19 per cent in 2009 to 19.2 per cent in 2010. The return on capital employed increased from 14 per cent in 2009 to 15.7 per cent in 2010. This indicates a healthy trend and the value of shares would further increase if this trend continues. The return is better than the return from risk-free investments of less than five per cent.

Proportion of shares owned ❻
The remaining 150,000 shares would give the purchaser 23 per cent ownership of the company. This amount added to shares already owned would bring the owner's shareholding close to the point of having to bid for the remainder of the shares.

Liquidity ❻
The acid test ratio improved from 0.9 to 0.95. This is a satisfactory position as the company now has 95c available to pay each €1 owed in the short term. The company does not have a liquidity problem.

Gearing ❻
The firm is low-geared. The gearing has improved from 40 per cent in 2009 to 37 per cent of total capital in 2010. Interest cover in 2009 was nine times and this cover has increased to 10 times in 2010. This indicates that there is little risk from creditors and a better prospect of higher dividends.

Sector ❻
The leisure industry is a growth industry. People are prepared to spend more of their disposable income on leisure.

aims

- To be able to prepare **final accounts** from partial information.
- To be able to distinguish **Type A** from **Type B** questions immediately.
- To be able to give relevant **advice** regarding these accounts.

Type A questions

To deal with Type A questions, look at them as an exercise in basic bookkeeping. First, enter the opening balances in general journal format to find the missing goodwill figure. Next enter all the figures in T accounts as opening balances. Then open a cash account and credit all the payments. Complete the double entry by debiting these accounts.

Do the same with the bank account – credit all the payments and then debit the other. The main problem areas in these questions arise with loans and interest calculations and with drawings. If the amount of the loan is funded, i.e. of an endowment type, then the total of the loan in the balance sheet will always be the original amount borrowed. If the loan is being repaid, then the amount of repayments made reduces the loan balance. Loan repayments do not go into the profit and loss account.

Type B questions

Don't try to tackle Type B questions in the same way as Type A. Instead, enter the opening figures in the general journal in order to find goodwill. Then enter the appropriate opening figures in the year-end balance sheet/statement of affairs. Find the closing

exam focus

When dealing with what are known as Type A questions – that is, cash/bank payment-type questions – it is a good idea to treat them as an exercise in basic bookkeeping.

key point

When allocating the figure for drawings for interest, light and heat, insurance, etc., you will be clearly instructed as to which way to calculate it – amount paid, amount used, amount payable, etc. By using the T account format and reading the instructions carefully, you will get the correct answer.

exam focus

In Type B questions, you have the same difficulties as in Type A regarding loans and drawings, but you go through the question in a different manner.

figures for stock, debtors, creditors, etc. and enter them in the balance sheet. Keep the number of accounts to a minimum, opening accounts only for expenses and drawings. Do not open a bank account.

Finally, the missing balance sheet figure will be the net profit which you will use in the profit and loss account to work back to the sales figure.

Question 3.1 (*Type A*)

On 1 January 2010 Eddie Dunphy purchased the business of Charlton & Co. for €125,000 consisting of the following tangible assets and liabilities: premises €99,000; stock €22,000; creditors €16,800; debtors €14,900; electricity due €540; and three months' insurance prepaid €1,500.

During 2010 Dunphy did not keep a full set of accounts but was able to supply you with the following information:

Cash payments: Purchases €43,400; general expenses €28,300; lodgements €53,000; light and heat €4,600.

Bank payments: Annual insurance premium €6,300; creditors €35,000; delivery van €18,000; interest €1,800; household furniture €5,600.

Bank lodgements: Lotto win €25,000; cash €53,000; debtors €27,500.

During the year Dunphy took from stock goods to the value of €250 per month and cash of €600 per month.

On 1 September 2010 he borrowed €80,000, part of which was used to purchase an adjoining premises for €72,000. The rate of interest was nine per cent per annum, payable monthly on the last day of each month. The capital sum was to be repaid in one lump sum in the year 2021, and to provide for this the bank was to pay €360 per month on the last day of each month into an investment account.

Dunphy estimated that one-third of light and heat used, insurance paid and interest payable should be attributed to the private section of the premises.

Included in the assets and liabilities of the business on 31 December 2010 were: creditors €16,400; stock €23,000; debtors €15,400; cash €680, electricity due €500, stock of heating oil €360; €25 interest earned by the fund to date.

You are required to:

(a) Prepare trading and profit and loss accounts for the year ended 31 December 2010.

(b) Prepare a balance sheet at 31 December 2010.

Solution to Question 3.1

(a)   E. Dunphy

Opening Entries
Method – Showing All Accounts

	Dr (€)	Cr (€)
Capital		125,000
Premises	99,000	
Stock	22,000	
Creditors		16,800
Debtors	14,900	
Electricity		540
Insurance	1,500	
Goodwill	4,940	
	142,340	142,340

Capital Account (1)

	(€)		(€)
		Opening Balance	125,000
		Bank	25,000

Premises Account (2)

	(€)		(€)
Opening Balance	99,000		
Loan	72,000		

Opening Stock (3)

	(€)		(€)
Opening Balance	22,000		

Total Creditors (4)

	(€)		(€)
Bank	35,000	Opening Balance	16,800
Balance	16,400	Credit Purchases	34,600
	51,400		51,400

Total Debtors (5)

	(€)		(€)
Opening Balance	14,900	Bank	27,500
Credit Sales	28,000	Balance	15,400
	42,900		42,900

Light and Heat Account (6)

	(€)		(€)
Cash	4,600	Opening Balance	540
Balance	500	Drawings	1,400
		Profit and Loss	2,800
		Balance	360
	5,100		5,100

Insurance Account (7)

	(€)		(€)
Opening Balance	1,500	Drawings	2,100
Bank	6,300	Profit and Loss	4,650
		Balance	1,050

Goodwill Account (8)

	(€)		(€)
Opening Balance	4,940		

Cash Account (9)

	(€)		(€)
Cash Sales	137,180	Purchases	43,400
		General Expenses	28,300
		Bank	53,000
		Light and Heat	4,600
		Drawings	7,200
		Balance	680
	137,180		137,180

Purchases Account (10)

	(€)		(€)
Cash	43,400	Drawings	3,000
Credit	34,600	Trading Account	75,000
	78,000		78,000

General Expenses (11)

	(€)		(€)
Cash	28,300		

Bank Account (12)

	(€)		(€)
Capital	25,000	Insurance	6,300
Cash	53,000	Creditors	35,000
Debtors	27,500	Delivery Vans	18,000
Loan	8,000	Interest	1,800
		Drawings	5,600
		Investment Fund	1,440
		Balance C/D	45,360
	113,500		113,500

Delivery Vans (13)

	(€)		(€)
Bank	18,000		

Interest (14)

	(€)		(€)
Bank	1,800	Drawings	800
Balance C/D	600	Profit and Loss	1,600
	2,400		2,400

Drawings (15)

	(€)		(€)
Bank	5,600		
Purchases	3,000		
Cash	7,200		
Light and Heat	1,400		
Interest	800		
Insurance	2,100		
	20,100		

Loan Account (16)

	(€)		(€)
		Premises	72,000
		Bank	8,000

Investment Fund Account (17)

	(€)		(€)
Bank	1,440		
Income	25		

Sales Account (18)

	(€)		(€)
Trading Account	165,180	Credit	28,000
		Cash	137,180
	165,180		165,180

Investment Income (19)

	(€)		(€)
		Fund	25

(b)   **Eddie Dunphy**

Trading and Profit and Loss Account for the Year Ended 31 December 2010

	(€)	(€)
Sales		165,180
Less Cost of Sales		
Opening Stock	22,000	
Purchases	75,000	
	97,000	
Less Closing Stock	23,000	
Cost of Sales		74,000
Gross Profit		91,180
Less Expenses		
Insurance	4,650	
General Expenses	28,300	
Light and Heat	2,800	
Interest	1,600	37,350
		53,830
Investment Income		25
Net Profit		53,855

Balance Sheet at 31 December 2010

	(€)	(€)	(€)
Fixed Assets			
Premises	171,000		
Delivery Vans	18,000		
Goodwill	4,940		
Investment Fund	1,465	195,405	
Current Assets			
Stock	23,000		
Debtors	15,400		
Bank	45,360		
Stock of Heating Oil	360		
Insurance Prepaid	1,050		
Cash	680		
		85,850	
Less Current Liabilities			
Creditors	16,400		
Interest	600		
Electricity Bill	500		
		17,500	68,350
Net Current Assets			263,755
Financed by			
Capital		150,000	
Plus Net Profit		53,855	
		203,855	
Less Drawings		20,100	
		183,755	
Loan		80,000	263,755

Question 3.2 (*Type B*)

On 1 January 2010 D. Swindler purchased a business for €110,000 consisting of the following tangible assets and liabilities: premises €86,000; stock €13,000; debtors €11,000; equipment €14,000; creditors €14,000; wages due €2,500; insurance prepaid €600.

During 2010 Swindler did not keep a full set of books but was able to supply you with the following information on 31 December 2010:

1. On 1 June 2010 Swindler borrowed €60,000 from International Finance Plc, some of which was used to purchase an adjoining premises for €56,000. It was agreed that Swindler would pay interest on the last day of each month at the rate of 11 per cent

per annum. The capital sum was to be repaid in one lump sum on 30 May 2025 and, to provide for this, the bank was to transfer €350 on the last day of each month into an investment account, commencing immediately.

2. Each week Swindler withdrew the following for personal use: stock €70 and cash €90.

3. During the year the following payments were made: insurance €2,400; wages €18,900; interest €3,300; motor vehicles €18,000; light and heat €4,450; sundry expenses €22,000. A €10,000 legacy was lodged to the business bank account.

4. Swindler estimated that one-third of the light and heat used, interest payable and insurance paid should be attributed to the private section of the premises. Two-thirds of the value of the motor vehicles was for private use.

5. Included in the assets and liabilities of the firm on 31 December 2010 were: stock €15,000; debtors €12,500; creditors €14,500; bank €17,000; electricity due €470; €40 interest earned by the fund to date.

6. Swindler's gross profit was 30 per cent of sales.

Prepare in as much detail as possible:

(a) Statement/balance sheet showing Swindler's profit/loss for the year.

(b) Trading and profit and loss accounts for the year.

(c) Advise Swindler.

exam focus

Don't be tempted to omit section (c) even when revising this topic. This is omitted by many students in examination.

Solution to Question 3.2

(a) General Journal

	Dr (€)	Cr (€)
Capital		110,000
Stock	13,000	
Premises	86,000	
Debtors	11,000	
Equipment	14,000	
Creditors		14,000
Wages Due		2,500
Insurance Prepaid	600	
Goodwill	1,900	
	126,500	126,500

Drawings

Purchases	3,640		
Cash	4,680		
Interest	1,283		
Motor Vehicles	12,000		
Insurance	800		
Light and Heat	1,640		
	24,043		

Wages Account

Bank	18,900	Balance	2,500
		Profit and Loss	16,400

Insurance Account*

Balance	600	Drawings	800
Bank	2,400	Profit and Loss	2,200
	3,000		3,000

*Should there be a balance on account at year-end?

Interest Account

Bank	3,300	Drawings	1,283
Balance	550	Profit and Loss	2,567
	3,850		3,850

Light & Heat

Bank	4,450	Drawings	1,640
Balance	470	Profit and Loss	3,280
	4,920		4,920

Loan 60,000 × 11% × 7/12 = 3,850

Balance Sheet at 31 December 2010

	(€)	(€)	(€)
Fixed Assets			
Premises (86,000 + 56,000)			142,000
Equipment			14,000
Motor Vehicles			6,000
Investment Fund (7 × 350) + 40			2,490
Goodwill			1,900
			166,390
Current Assets			
Stock		15,000	
Debtors		12,500	
Bank		17,000	
		44,500	
Less Current Liabilities			
Creditors	14,500		
ESB Bill	470		
Interest	550		
	15,520	28,980	
Net Current Assets			195,370
Financed by			
Capital (110,000 + 10,000)		120,000	
Plus Net Profit		39,413	
Less Drawings		(24,043)	
Term Loan		60,000	195,370

(b) Trading and Profit and Loss Accounts for the Year Ended 31 December 2010

	(€)	(€)
Sales		286,067
Less Cost of Sales		
Opening Stock	13,000	
Purchases (205,887 – 3,640)	202,247	
	215,247	
Less Closing Stock	15,000	
Cost of Sales		200,247
Gross Profit		85,820
Less Expenses		
Wages	16,400	
Insurance	2,200	
Insurance	2,567	
Light and Heat	3,280	
Sundry Expenses	22,000	46,447
		39,373
Plus Fund Income		40
Net Profit		39,413

(c) Swindler should keep all appropriate subsidiary books. Proper ledger accounts would eliminate the need to rely on estimates.

Question 3.3

On 1/1/2009 R. Roberts purchased a business for €210,000 consisting of the following tangible assets and liabilities: premises €180,000, stock €16,400, debtors €14,000, three months' premises insurance prepaid €900, trade creditors €20,400, and wages due €2,400.

During 2009 Roberts did not keep a full set of accounts but was able to supply the following information on 31/12/2009:

Cash payments: Lodgements €104,000, general expenses €32,300, purchases €86,200.

Bank payments: Delivery vans €33,200, creditors €42,200, light and heat €6,400, interest €2,475, annual premises insurance premium €4,800, covenant for charitable organisation €2,000, furniture €16,000.

Bank lodgements: Debtors €35,000, cash €104,000, dividends €4,500.

Roberts took from stock goods to the value of €90 and cash €100 per week for household use during the year. Roberts borrowed €90,000 on 1/9/2009, part of which was used to purchase an adjoining premises costing €75,000. It was agreed that Roberts would pay interest on the last day of each month at the rate of 11 per cent per annum. The capital sum was to be repaid in a lump sum in the year 2017 and to provide for this the bank was to transfer €600 on the last day of each month from Roberts' bank account into an investment fund. Roberts estimated that 25 per cent of furniture and light and heat used as well as 20 per cent of interest payable for the year should be attributed to the private section of the premises.

Included in the assets and liabilities of the firm on 31/12/2009 were stock €18,300, debtors €22,500, trade creditors €34,800, cash €600, electricity due €560, and €66 interest earned by the fund to date.

You are required to show, with workings:

(a) Trading, profit and loss account for the year ended 31/12/2009. `60`

(b) Balance sheet as at 31/12/2009. `40`

`100 marks`

Solution to Question 3.3

(a) Trading and Profit and Loss Account for Year Ended 31 December 2009

	Workings	€	€	€
Sales	W1			271,800 ⑩
Less Cost of Sales				
Stock at 1 January 2009			16,400 ❸	
Add Purchases	W2		138,120 ❽	
			154,520	
Less Stock 31 December 2009			18,300 ❸	136,220
Gross Profit				135,580

Less Expenses

General Expenses	W3	29,900 ❺	
Covenant		2,000 ❶	
Insurance	W4	4,500 ❼	
Interest	W5	2,640 ❼	
Light and Heat	W6	5,220 ❼	44,260
			91,320
Add Income from Investment Fund			66 ❷
Net Profit			91,386 ❼

(b) Balance Sheet as at 31 December 2009

	€	€	€
Intangible Fixed Assets			
Goodwill		21,500 ❷	
Tangible Fixed Assets			
Buildings		255,000 ❶	
Delivery Vans		33,200 ❶	
Furniture		12,000 ❶	321,700
Investments			2,466 ❺
			324,166
Current Assets			
Stock at 31 December 2009	18,300 ❶		
Trade Debtors	22,500 ❶		
Bank W7	49,025 ❽		
Cash	600 ❶		
Prepayment (Insurance)	1,200 ❸	91,625	
Less Creditors: Amounts Falling Due within One Year			
Creditors	34,800 ❶		
Interest Due	825 ❷		
Electricity Due	560 ❶	36,185	55,440
			379,606 ❸
Financed by			
Creditors: Amounts Falling Due after More than One Year			
Loan			90,000 ❶
Capital – Balance at 1/1/2009	210,000 ❶		
Add Capital Introduced	4,500 ❷		
Add Net Profit	91,386	305,886	
Less Drawings W8		16,280 ❽	289,606
Capital Employed			379,606

Workings

1. Sales

Payments by Debtors	35,000	
Amount Owed by Debtors 31/12/2009	22,500	
	57,500	
Less Amount Owed on 1/1/2009	14,000	
Credit Sales	43,500	
Cash Sales (104,000 + 32,300 + 86,200 + 600 + 5,200)	228,300	271,800

2. Purchases

Payments to Creditors	42,200	
Creditors at 31/12/2009	34,800	
	77,000	
Less Creditors at 1/1/2009	20,400	
Credit Purchases	56,600	
Cash Purchases	86,200	
Total Purchases	142,800	
Less Drawings – Goods	4,680	138,120

3. General Expenses

Amount Paid	32,300	
Less Wages Due 1/1/2009	(2,400)	29,900

4. Insurance

Amount Paid	2,450	
Add Insurance Prepaid 1/1/2009	900	
Less Insurance Prepaid 31/12/2009	(1,200)	4,500

5. Interest for Year (4/12 × 79,900)

Interest Paid	2,475	
Interest Due 31/12/2009	825	
	3,300	
Less Drawings (1/5)	660	2,640

6. Light and Heat

Amount Paid	6,400	
Add Electricity Due 31/12/2009	560	
Less Drawings (1/3)	(1,740)	5,220

7. Bank

Receipts

Lodgements	104,000	
Debtors	35,000	
Capital/Dividends	4,500	
Loan	90,000	233,500

Less Payments

Creditors	42,200	
Insurance	4,800	
Light and Heat	6,400	
Furniture	16,000	
Vans	33,200	
Covenant	2,000	
Interest	2,475	
Investment (4 × 600)	2,400	
Buildings	75,000	184,475
Balance		49,025

8. **Drawings**

Furniture	4,000
Drawings of Cash	4,680
Drawing of Goods	5,200
Interest	660
Light and Heat	1,740
Total	16,280

9. **Goodwill Account**

Assets			Liabilities		
	Premises	180,000		Creditors	20,400
	Stock	16,400		Wages Due	2,400
	Debtors	14,000		Capital	210,000
	Insurance Prepaid	900			
		211,300			
	Missing Figure – Goodwill	21,500			
		232,800			232,800

Question 3.4

J. O'Higgins lodged €350,000 to a business bank account on 1/1/2010 and on the same day purchased a business for €320,000, including the following assets and liabilities: buildings €290,000, stock €16,700, three months' rates prepaid €2,400, debtors €32,500, wages due €3,600 and trade creditors €58,000.

O'Higgins did not keep a full set of books during 2010 but estimates that the gross profit was 40 per cent of sales and was able to supply the following additional information on 31/12/2010:

1. Each week O'Higgins took from stock goods to the value of €100 and cash €150 for household expenses.

2. On 1/10/2010 O'Higgins borrowed €300,000, part of which was used to purchase an adjoining premises costing €250,000. It was agreed that O'Higgins would pay interest on the last day of the month at the rate of six per cent per annum. The capital sum was to be repaid in one lump sum in the year 2018 and, to provide for

this, the bank was instructed to transfer €2,500 on the last day of every month from O'Higgins's business account into an investment fund.

3. During the year, O'Higgins lodged dividends €2,500 to the business bank and made the following payments: light and heat €7,200, interest €3,000, wages and general expenses €98,000, equipment €16,000, rates for 12 months €10,800, and college fees €4,500.

4. O'Higgins estimated that 25 per cent of the equipment, light and heat *used* and interest *payable* should be attributed to the private section of the premises. O'Higgins further estimated that 70 per cent of college fees should be attributed to a family member and the remainder to an employee.

5. Included in the assets and liabilities of the firm on 31/12/2010 were stock €17,200, debtors €34,300, trade creditors €29,900, cash at bank €68,462, electricity due €560 and €75 interest earned by the investment fund to date.

You are required to prepare, with workings:

(a) Statement/balance sheet showing O'Higgins's profit or loss for the year ended 31/12/2010.   50

(b) Trading, profit and loss account, in as much detail as possible, for the year ended 31/12/2010.   40

(c) Summary of the advice you would give to O'Higgins in relation to the information given above.   10

100 marks

Solution to Question 3.4

(a) Balance Sheet as at 31 December 2010   50

	€	€
Intangible Assets		
Goodwill		40,000 ❸
Fixed Assets		
Buildings (290,000 + 250,000)	54,000 ❸	
Equipment	12,000 ❸	552,000
Financial Assets		
Investments		7,575 ❹
		599,575
Current Assets		
Stock at 31 December 2010	17,200 ❶	
Trade Debtors	34,300 ❶	
Bank	68,462 ❶	
Rates Prepaid	2,700 ❹	122,662

Less Creditors: Amounts Falling Due within One Year

Creditors	29,900 ❶		
Interest Due	1,500 ❸		
Electricity Due	560 ❷	(31,960)	
Working Capital			90,702
			690,277

Financed by

Creditors: Amounts Falling Due after More than One Year

Loan			300,000 ❷
Capital – Balance at 1/1/2008		350,000 ❷	
Add Capital Introduced		2,500 ❸	
Less Drawings	W10	(23,215) ❿	329,285
			629,285
Add Net Profit	W1		60,992
Capital Employed			690,277 ❼

(b) Trading and Profit and Loss Account for Year Ended 31 December 2008 **40**

		€	€
Sales	W3		440,905 ❷
Less Cost of Goods Sold			
Stock at 1 January 2008		16,700 ❷	
Add Purchases (270,243 − 5,200)	W5	265,043 ❷	
		281,743	
Less Stock 31 December 2008		(17,200) ❷	
Cost of Sales	W4		264,543 ❷
Gross Profit	W2		176,362 ❷
Add Investment Income			75 ❸
			176,437
Less Expenses			
Wages and General Expenses	W6	95,750 ❻	
Light and Heat	W7	5,820 ❻	
Rates	W8	10,500 ❻	
Interest	W9	3,375 ❻	115,445
Net Profit	W1		60,992 ❶

(c) **10**

O'Higgins should keep a detailed cash book and general ledger supported by appropriate subsidiary day books. This would enable O'Higgins to prepare an accurate trading and profit and loss account and therefore would avoid reliance on estimates.

Workings

	€	€
1. **Net Profit for Year (Balancing Figure in Balance Sheet)**		
Total Net Assets	690,277	
Less Loan	(300,000)	
Less Capital after Drawings and before Profit	(329,285)	60,992
2. **Gross Profit**		
Net Profit + Expenses – Gains = (60,987 + 115,450 – 75)		175,362
3. **Sales**		
Gross Profit = 40% of sales = 176,362 × 2.5		440,905
4. **Cost of Sales**		
Sales Less Gross Profit = 440,905 – 176,362		264,543
5. **Purchases**		
Cost of Sales + Closing Stock – Opening Stock 264,543 + 17,200 – 16,700		265,043
6. **Wages and General Expenses** – Amount Paid	98,000	
Add College Fees 30% of 74,500	1,350	
Less Wages Due at 1/1/2008	(3,600)	95,750
7. **Light and Heat** – Amount Paid	7,200	
Add Electricity Due 31/12/2010	560	
Less Drawings	(1,940)	
Profit and Loss Account		5,820
8. **Rates** – Amount Paid	10,800	
Add Rates Prepaid 1/1/2010	2,400	
Less Rates Prepaid 31/12/2010	(2,700)	
Profit and Loss Account		10,500
9. **Interest** – Amount Paid	3,000	
Add Interest Due	1,500	
Less Drawings	(1,125)	
Profit and Loss Account		3,375
10. **Drawings**		
College Fees – Family Member	3,150	
Equipment	4,000	
Drawings of Stock	5,200	
Cash	7,800	
Light and Heat	1,940	
Interest	1,125	23,215

4 Club Accounts

The first set of figures must be entered twice, once in the calculation of the accumulated fund and secondly either in the income and expenditure a/c or the balance sheet. Deal with both of these first – e.g. Clubhouse and Courts, a fixed asset, is a debit in the accumulated fund calculation and, of course, a fixed asset in the balance sheet.

The receipts and payments figures are entered once. Many of the receipts are incomes and many of the payments are expenditures.

The final items are then entered twice.

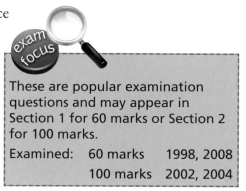

exam focus

These are popular examination questions and may appear in Section 1 for 60 marks or Section 2 for 100 marks.

Examined: 60 marks   1998, 2008
            100 marks   2002, 2004

key point

Watch out for these:

- Bar sales = receipts − opening debtors + closing debtors.
- Bar purchases = cash purchases − opening creditors + closing creditors.
- Subscriptions prepaid at beginning of year belong to this year and at end of year belong to next year. They are both current liabilities.
- Life membership and levy collected during the year are both subtracted from subscriptions and included in reserves. A portion of the life membership is then put back into income. Levy due at beginning of year is a current asset.
- Loan calculations are also tricky.

  e.g. Repaid €40,000 loan on 30/06/ – together with 18 months' interest totalling €43,600.

  18 months' interest = €3,600

  1 month's interest = €200

  1 year's interest = €2,400

  due at beginning of year

  6 months' interest = €1,200 expenditure

- If repayment date were 31/12/ – then the interest figures would be inverted.

Question 4.1

Included in the assets and liabilities of the Love All Tennis Club on 1 January 2010 were the following: clubhouse and land €190,000; equipment at cost €7,500; bar stock €8,000; subscriptions in advance €500; bar debtors €350; bar creditors €3,200; affiliation fees due €300.

The club treasurer has supplied the following account of the club's activities for the year ended 31 December 2010.

Receipts	(€)	Payments	(€)
Bank Current Account	10,000	Sundry Expenses	14,500
Bar Receipts	78,000	Bar Purchases	57,000
Subscriptions	43,500	Affiliation Fees	900
Disposal of Equipment (cost €2,000)	800	Competition Prizes	1,100
Interest from 6% Government		Catering Costs	3,100
Investment of €15,000	1,350	Purchase of 7% Government	
Catering Receipts	4,600	Bonds on 31 August 2010	12,000
Competition Receipts	600	Transfer to Deposit Account	
		on 31 December 2010	10,000
		Purchase of Prize Bonds	200
		Repayment of €14,000 Loan	
		on 30 June 2010 with	
		1.5 years' interest	16,520
		Balance	23,530
	138,850		138,850

You are given the following additional information:

1. Bar stock on 31 December 2010 is €8,800.
2. Subscriptions include three life memberships of €800 each, and there are subscriptions due of €500.
3. Equipment at 31 December 2010 is to be depreciated at the rate of 20 per cent per annum.
4. Bar debtors and creditors are €360 and €3,400, respectively.
5. Life membership is to be credited to income over a five-year period beginning in 2010.

Prepare the following:

(a) A statement of accumulated fund at 1 January 2010.

(b) An income and expenditure account for the year ended 31 December 2010.

(c) A balance sheet at 31 December 2010.

(d) A report to the members on the advisability of purchasing a piece of land adjoining their property that has come on the market at €200,000.

Solution to Question 4.1

The Love All Tennis Club
(a) Accumulated Fund on 1 January 2010

	Dr (€)	Cr (€)
Clubhouse and Land	190,000	
Equipment	7,500	
Bar Stock	8,000	
Subscriptions in Advance		500
Bar Debtors	350	
Bar Creditors		3,200
Affiliation Fees Due		300
Bank	10,000	
6% Government Investment	15,000	
6% Investment Income Due	450	
Loan		14,000
Interest Due		1,680
Accumulated Fund		211,620
	231,300	231,300

(b) Income and Expenditure Account for the Year Ended 31 December 2010

	Workings		(€)
Income			
Bar Profit	W1	21,610	
Subscriptions	W2	42,100	
Catering Profit (4,600 – 3,100)		1,500	
6% Investment Income		900	
7% Investment Income		280	
Life Membership		480	66,870
Expenditure			
Sundry Expenses		14,500	
Affiliation Fees (900 – 300)		600	
Loss on Competitions (1,100 – 600)		500	
Interest		840	
Loss on Disposal of Equipment		1,200	
Depreciation of Equipment		1,100	18,740
Excess of Income			48,130

Workings

W1   **Bar Trading Account**

		(€)
Sales (78,000 − 350 + 360)		78,010
Less Cost of Opening Stock	8,000	
Add Purchases (57,000 − 3,200 + 3,400)	57,200	
	65,200	
Less Closing Stock	8,800	
Cost		56,400
Gross Profit		21,610

W2   **Subscriptions 43,500 + 500 − 2,400 + 500 = 42,100**

	(€)
Life Membership	2,400
Income	480
Reserves	1,920

(c) Balance Sheet at 31 December 2010

	Cost (€)	Accumulated Depreciation (€)	Net (€)
Fixed Assets			
Clubhouse and Land	190,000		190,000
Equipment	5,500	1,100	4,400
	195,500	1,100	194,400
6% Government Stock			15,000
Prize Bonds			200
7% Government Bonds			12,000
			221,600
Current Assets			
Bank	23,530		
Closing Stock	8,800		
Bar Debtors	360		
Deposit Account	10,000		
Subscriptions Due	500		
Income Due on 7% Bond	280		

	43,470	
Less Current Liabilities/Creditors	3,400	40,070
		261,670
Financed by		
Accumulated Fund	211,620	
Excess of Income	48,130	
Life Membership	1,920	
		261,670

(d)

Points in favour of purchase: The club has liquid assets of government investments €27,000; deposit account €10,000; current account €23,530. In addition:

- It has repaid its loan.
- It could levy its members.
- It could offer reduced life membership (which might reduce its future income).
- It could apply for lottery funding.
- It could finance some borrowing.

Points against purchase:

- The land might not be suitable for development.
- There may be planning permission problems.
- Development costs may be very high.
- The club may have a burden of interest/loan repayments in the future.

Question 4.2

Included in the assets and liabilities of the Below Par Golf Club at 1 January 2010 were the following: clubhouse and land €180,000; life membership €18,000; equipment at book value €17,000; bar debtors €250; bar creditors €5,600; levy reserve fund €40,000, bar stock €6,600.

The club treasurer has supplied the following information regarding the club's activities during the year ended 31 December 2010.

Receipts	(€)	Payments	(€)
Bank Current Account	12,000	Catering Expenses	3,400
Interest from 7% Government		Sundry Expenses	24,000
Investments 2009	2,100	Greenkeepers' Wages	15,900

Interest from 7% Government Investments 2010	2,100	Bar Purchases	56,750
Catering Receipts	5,800	Repayment of €30,000 Loan on 30 September 2002 with 2.5 Years' Interest	38,000
Bar Receipts	84,600	Equipment	9,000
Subscriptions	96,300	Transfer to Deposit Account on 31 December 2010	20,000
		Balance	35,850
	202,900		202,900

You are given the following additional information:

1. Bar stock is €6,900.
2. Equipment owned at 31 December 2010 is valued at €23,500.
3. Subscriptions include the following: two life memberships, which bring the total to 14, a levy for the year of €50 on 400 members and a levy of €50 on 10 members which has been pending since last year.
4. Debtors and creditors are €300 and €5,500, respectively.
5. Greenkeepers' wages due are €1,400.

Prepare the following:

(a) A statement of accumulated fund at 1 January 2010.

(b) An income and expenditure account for the year ended 31 December 2010.

(c) A balance sheet at 31 December 2010.

(d) A report to the members on funding a €100,000 extension.

Solution to Question 4.2

Below Par Golf Club
(a) Accumulated Fund on 1 January 2010

	Workings	Dr (€)	Cr (€)
Clubhouse and Land		180,000	
Life Membership			18,000
Equipment (net)		1,700	
Bar Debtors		250	
Bar Creditors			5,600
Levy Reserve Fund			40,000
Bar Stock		6,600	
Bank		12,000	
7% Investments		30,000	

Investment Income Due		2,100	
Levy Fund Due		500	
Loan	W3		30,000
Interest Due	W3		5,600
Accumulated Fund			149,250
		248,450	248,450

(b) Income and Expenditure Account for the Year Ended 31 December 2010

	Workings	(€)	(€)
Income			
Bar Profit	W1	28,300	
7% Investment Income		2,100	
Catering Profit (5,800 – 3,400)		2,400	
Subscriptions	W2	72,800	105,600
Expenditure			
Sundry Expenses		24,000	
Greenkeepers' Wages (15,900 + 1,400)		17,300	
Loan Interest	W3	2,400	
Depreciation – Equipment		2,500	46,200
Excess of Income			59,400

Workings

W1: Bar Trading Account

	(€)	(€)
Sales (84,600 – 250 + 300)		84,650
Less Cost		
Opening Stock	6,600	
Add Purchases (56,750 – 5,600 + 5,500)	56,650	
	63,250	
Less Closing Stock	6,900	
Cost of Sales		56,350
Profit		28,300

W2: Subscriptions

	(€)
Subscriptions	96,300
Life	(3,000)
Levy	(20,000)
Levy	(500)
	72,800

W3: Loan

	(€)
Repaid	38,000
Loan	30,000
Total Interest	8,000
0.5 Year's Interest	1,600
1 Year's Interest	3,200
9 Months' Interest	2,400
Interest Due	5,600

(c) Balance Sheet at 31 December 2010

	Cost (€)	Account Depreciation (€)	Net (€)
Fixed Assets			
Clubhouse and Land	180,000		180,000
Equipment	26,000	2,500	23,500
	206,000	2,500	203,500
7% Investments (or C/A)			30,000
Current Assets			
Stock	6,900		
Debtors	300		
Bank	35,850		
Deposit Account	20,000		
		63,050	
Less Current Liabilities			
Creditors	5,500		
Greenkeepers' Wages	1,400	6,900	56,150
			289,650
Enhanced by			
Accumulated Fund			149,250
Excess of Income			59,400
Levy Reserve Fund			60,000
Life Membership			21,000
			289,650

(d)

Don't wait two years. Why:

- 35,850 in current account
- 20,000 in deposit account
- 30,000 in investment fund
- Loan paid off
- Lottery funding?

Question 4.3

Included in the assets and liabilities of the Nokemdown Indoor and Outdoor Bowling Club on 1 January 2010 were the following: clubhouse and land €285,000; equipment €28,000; bar stock €16,000; life membership €30,000; bar debtors €130; bar creditors €4,300; levy reserve fund €16,000; six per cent investment income due €300; wages due €200.

The club treasurer has supplied the following information for the year ended 31 December 2010:

Receipts	(€)	Payments	(€)
Catering Receipts	7,600	Bar Current Account	4,560
Annual Grant	5,500	Equipment	9,000
Subscriptions	53,200	Catering Costs	8,300
Interest from 6% Investments	1,800	Wages	15,200
Bar Receipts	72,600	General Expenses	24,000
Sale of Equipment	1,600	Bar Purchases	61,000
		Repayment of €16,000 Loan on 30 September 2010 with 2.25 Years' Interest	19,600
		Balance	540
	142,200		142,200

You are also given the following information:

1. Bar stock on 31 December 2010 is €16,500.
2. Subscriptions include the following:
   - (a) Three life memberships, bringing the total to 63.
   - (b) Levy for 2010 is 400 members at 740.
   - (c) Levy from five members for 2009.
   - (d) Subscriptions due €400.
3. Bar debtors and creditors are €150 and €4,800, respectively.
4. Book value of equipment €31,000.

Prepare the following:

(a) A statement of accumulated fund at 1 January 2010.

(b) An income and expenditure account for the year ended 31 December 2010.

(c) A balance sheet at 31 December 2010.

Solution to Question 4.3

(a) Nokemdown Indoor and Outdoor Bowling Club Accumulated Fund 1 January 2010

	Dr (€)	Cr (€)
Clubhouse and Land	285,000	
Equipment	28,000	
Bar Stock	16,000	
Life Membership		30,000
Bar Debtors	130	
Bar Creditors		4,300
Levy Reserve Fund		16,000
Investment Income Due	300	
Wages Due		200
Bank		4,560
6% Investments	25,000	
Levy Fund Due	200	
Loan		16,000
Interest Due		2,400
Accumulated Fund	_____	281,170
	354,630	354,630

Workings

W1: Subscriptions

	(€)
Subscriptions	53,200
Life Membership	(1,500)
Levy 2010	(16,000)
Levy 2009	(200)
Due	400
	35,900

W2: Bar Trading Account

		(€)
Sales (72,600 − 130 + 150)		72,620
Less Cost Opening Stock	16,000	
Purchases		
(61,000 − 4,300 + 4,800)	61,500	
	77,500	
Less Closing Stock	16,500	
Cost of Sales		61,000
Profit		11,620

W3: Equipment Depreciation

Equipment $(28,000 - 1,600 + 900) = 35,400$
Value 31 December 2007 = <u>31,000</u>
Depreciation = 4,400

(b) Income and Expenditure Account for the Year Ended 31 December 2010

	Workings	(€)	(€)
Income			
Annual Grant		5,500	
Subscriptions	W1	35,900	
Investment Income		1,500	
Bar Profit	W2	11,620	54,520
Expenditure			
Catering Loss (8,300 – 7,500)		800	
Wages (15,200 – 200)		15,000	
General Expenses		24,000	
Loan Interest		1,200	
Depreciation – Equipment	W3	4,400	45,400
Excess of Income			9,120

(c) Balance Sheet at 31 December 2010

	Cost (€)	Accumulated Depreciation (€)	Net (€)
Fixed Assets			
Clubhouse and Land	285,000		285,000
Equipment	35,400	4,400	31,000
	320,400	4,400	316,000
Current Assets			
Bar Stock	16,500		
Bar Debtors	150		
Bank	540		
6% Investments	2,500		
Subs Due	400		
	42,590		

Less Current Liabilities		
Creditors	4,800	
Net Current Assets		37,790
		353,790
Financed by		
Accumulated Fund	281,170	
Excess of Income	9,120	
Levy Reserve Fund	32,000	
Life Membership	31,500	
		353,790

Question 4.4

Included among the assets and liabilities of the Green Glen Golf Club on 1/1/2010 were the following: clubhouse and course €740,000, bar stock €3,800, equipment (at cost) €28,600, life membership €36,000, bar debtors €155, bar creditors €2,450, subscriptions received in advance €1,800, six per cent government investments €40,000, investment income due €150, levy reserve fund €60,000 and wages due €2,400.

The club treasurer has supplied the following account of the club's activities during the year ended 31/12/2010:

Receipts	€	Payments	€
Bank Current Account	4,440	Bar Purchases	80,500
Investment Income	1,450	Sundry Expenses	185,600
Entrance Fees	17,000	Catering Costs	4,460
Catering Receipts	6,650	Equipment	44,500
Annual Sponsorship	33,000	Coaching Lessons	4,650
Subscriptions	254,200	Repayment of €30,000 Loan	
Bar Receipts	112,660	on 31/12/2009 together	
		with 1.25 Years' Interest	34,500
		Transfer to Building Society	
		31/12/2009	70,000
		Balance	5,190
	€429,400		€429,400

You are given the following additional information and instructions:
1. Bar stock on 31/12/2010 was €4,300.
2. Equipment owned on 31/12/2010 is to be depreciated at the rate of 20 per cent of cost.
3. Clubhouse and course to be depreciated by two per cent of cost.
4. Bar debtors and bar creditors on 31/12/2010 were €110 and €2,770, respectively.

5. Subscriptions include:

    (a) Two life memberships of €6,000 each.

    (b) Subscriptions for 2010 amounting to €2,400.

    (c) Levy for 2009 of €200 on 300 members.

    (d) Levy of €200 on eight members for 2009.

6. Life membership was to be written off over a 12-year period commencing in 2010.

You are required to:

(a) Show the club's accumulated fund (capital) on 1/1/2010.   `30`

(b) Show the income and expenditure account for the year ended 31/12/2010.   `35`

(c) Show the club's balance sheet on 31/12/2010.   `20`

(d) Indicate the points you, as treasurer, might make if the members at the AGM of the club proposed to reduce the annual subscription by 20 per cent.   `15`

`100 marks`

Solution to Question 4.4

(a) Accumulated Fund at 1 January 2010   `30`

	€	€
Assets		
Clubhouse and Course	740,000 ❶	
Bar Stock	3,800 ❶	
Equipment	28,600 ❶	
Bar Debtors	155 ❶	
6% Government Investments	40,000 ❷	
Interest on Investments	150 ❷	
Levy Due	1,600 ❸	
Bank Current Account	4,440 ❸	818,745
Less Liabilities		
Life Membership	36,000 ❷	
Creditors	2,450 ❶	
Subscriptions Prepaid	1,800 ❷	
Levy Reserve Fund	60,000 ❷	
Wages Due	2,400 ❶	
Loan	30,000 ❷	
Loan Interest Due	900 ❸	133,550
Accumulated Fund/Capital at 1 January 2010 ❶		685,195 ❷

(b) Income and Expenditure Account for the Year Ended 31 December 2010 `35`

		€	€
Income			
Bar Profit	W1	32,295 ❻	
Investment Income	W2	2,400 ❸	
Subscriptions	W3	180,000 ❻	
Life Membership	W4	4,000 ❸	
Entrance Fees		17,000 ❶	
Annual Sponsorship		33,000 ❶	
Profit from Catering	W5	2,190 ❷	270,885
Less Expenditure			
Sundry Expenses (185,600 – 2,400)		183,200 ❸	
Loan Interest		3,600 ❷	
Depreciation – Equipment		14,620 ❷	
Depreciation – Clubhouse and Courts		14,800 ❷	
Coaching Lessons		4,650 ❶	220,870
Surplus of Income over Expenditure for Year			50,015 ❸

(c) Balance Sheet as at 31/12/2010 `20`

	Cost €	Dep to date €	NBV €
Fixed Assets			
Clubhouse and Courts	740,000 ❶	14,800 ❶	725,200
Equipment	73,100 ❷	14,620 ❶	58,480
	813,100	29,420	783,680
Investments			
6% Government Investments		40,000 ❶	
Building Society		70,000 ❶	110,000
			893,680
Current Assets			
Bar Stock		4,300 ❶	
Bar Debtors		110 ❶	
Investment Income Due		1,100 ❸	
Bank		5,190 ❶	
		10,700	

Less Creditors: Amounts Falling Due within One Year			
Subscriptions Prepaid	2,400 ❶		
Bar Creditors	2,770 ❶	5,170	
Working Capital			5,530
Total Net Assets			899,210
Financed by			
Creditors: Amounts Falling Due after More than One Year			
Life Membership			44,000 ❷
Levy Reserve Fund			120,000 ❷
Accumulated Fund			
Balance at 1 January 2010		685,195 ❶	
Add Excess of Income for Year		50,015	735,210
Capital Employed			899,210

(d) 15

A reduction in subscriptions of 20 per cent for 2011 would involve a reduction in club income of €36,000. ❻

Although the club is financially sound as it has €5,190 in the bank, €70,000 in the building society, investments worth €40,000 and has paid off a loan of €30,000, these funds are set aside for future capital expenditure. ❸

The club's surplus of income for the year 2010 of €50,015 would seem to indicate that the club is capable of bearing a reduction of 20 per cent. However, almost all of this surplus is provided by entrance fees of €17,000 and sponsorship of €33,000 and this income cannot be guaranteed in future years. ❸

It can be argued that a reduction in membership fees could attract more members and thus bring in entrance fees as well as increased bar profit. However, it would *not* be prudent to reduce subscription fees at present and instead it would be advisable to retain the present level of fees and use these fees to provide improved facilities for the members and thus attract more members. ❸

Workings

1. **Bar Profit – Bar Trading Account for Year Ended 31/12/2010**

	€	€
Sales (112,660 − 155 + 110)		112,615
Less Cost of Goods Sold		
Stock at 1 January 2010	3,800	
Add Purchases (80,500 + 2,770 − 2,450)	80,820	
Less Stock 31 December 2010	(4,300)	80,320
Bar Profit		32,295

2. **Investment Income**

	€	
Income Received	1,450	
Less Income Due 1/1/2010	(150)	
Add Income Due 31/12/2010	1,100	
Income and Expenditure Account		2,400

3. **Subscriptions**

	€	
Subscriptions Received	254,200	
Add Subscriptions Prepaid at 1/1/2010	1,800	
Less Subscriptions Prepaid at 31/12/2010	(2,400)	
Less Levy for 2010	(60,000)	
Less Levy for 2009	(1,600)	
Less Two Life Memberships	(12,000)	
Income and Expenditure Account		180,000

4. **Life Membership** 1/1/2010

	€	
Life Membership 1/1/2010	36,000	
Add Membership Received	12,000	
Less Amount Transferred to I & E Account	(4,000)	
Balance 31/12/2010		44,000

5. **Profit on Catering** – Catering Receipts

	€	
Profit on Catering – Catering Receipts	6,650	
Catering Costs	4,460	
Income and Expenditure Account		2,190

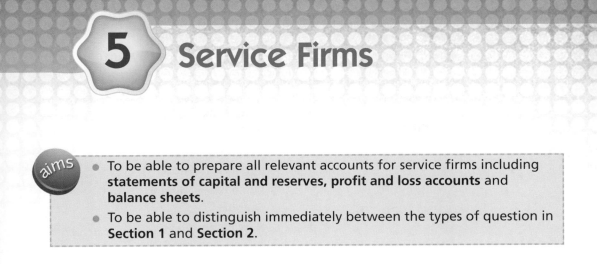

aims

- To be able to prepare all relevant accounts for service firms including **statements of capital and reserves, profit and loss accounts** and **balance sheets**.
- To be able to distinguish immediately between the types of question in **Section 1** and **Section 2**.

There is a slight difference between the questions in Section 1 and Section 2. In section 1 the questions are for a sole practitioner and you are asked to prepare a profit and loss account and balance sheet.

In section 2 the questions are for a limited company – maybe a health centre – and you are asked to calculate the company's reserves at the beginning of the year, to prepare a subsidiary trading and profit and loss account, the main profit and loss account and the balance sheet.

key point

The main point of difference in these questions is the issue of accumulated depreciation. The fixed assets will have a number of years' accumulated depreciation which is not included in the list of given figures. These should be calculated immediately multiplying the number of years by the relevant percentage.

exam focus

The approach to both of these questions is similar to club accounts and incomplete records. These should be laid out blank on four separate pages. Make sure to show all workings.

Question 5.1

Included in the assets and liabilities of the Looking Good Health Centre on 1/1/2010 were the following: buildings and grounds at cost €850,000; equipment at cost €80,000; furniture at cost €30,000; stock of health food €1,800; stock of heating oil €700; contract cleaning prepaid €400; creditors for supplies €2,100; clients' fees paid in advance €6,000; investments €100,000; authorised capital €950,000; issued capital €650,000. All fixed assets have two years' accumulated depreciation on 1/1/2010.

Receipts and Payments Account for the Year Ending 31/12/2010

Receipts	€	Payments	€
Current a/c 1/1/2010	8,600	Wages and Salaries	90,150
Clients' Fees	251,500	Insurance	6,300
Interest	2,500	Light and Heat	3,200
Shop Receipts	72,400	Purchases – Shop	39,500
		Purchases – Supplies	27,800
		Laundry	3,600
		New Extension 1/1/2010	50,000
		Contract Cleaning	2,900
		Telephone and Postage	1,900
		Equipment 1/1/2010	18,000
		Repayment of €70,000 Loan on 30/6/2010 with 18 Months' Interest	76,000
		Balance	15,650
	335,000		335,000

You are given the following additional information:

1. Closing stock: shop €1,900; heating oil €400.
2. Electricity due 31/12/2010 €300.
3. Contract cleaning prepaid €500.
4. Clients' fees prepaid €3,000. Fees in arrears €2,000.
5. Wages and salaries include €18,000 paid to the receptionist who also runs the shop. It is estimated that 50 per cent of this salary and €300 of the light and heat, €500 of the insurance and €400 of the telephone is attributable to the shop.
6. The health centre revalued the buildings and grounds at €950,000 on 31/12/2010.
7. Depreciation is to be provided as follows:
   Buildings – two per cent of cost for a full year.
   Equipment – 20 per cent of cost per annum.
   Furniture – 20 per cent of cost per annum.
8. Creditors for supplies €1,700.

You are required to prepare all the accounts.

Solution to Question 5.1

Looking Good Health Centre

Reserves at 1/1/2010	Dr €	Cr €
Buildings and Grounds	850,000	
Acc Depn.: Buildings		34,000
Equipment	80,000	
Acc Depn.: Equipment		32,000
Furniture	30,000	
Acc Depn.: Furniture		12,000
Stock: Health Food	1,800	
Stock: Heating Oil	700	
Contract Cleaning Prepaid	400	
Creditors for Supplies		2,100
Clients' Fees in Advance		6,000
Investments	100,000	
Share Capital (950,000)		650,000
Bank	8,600	
Loan		70,000
Interest		4,000
Reserves at 1/1/2010		261,400
	1,071,500	1,071,500

Health Shop Profit and Loss Account for the Year Ending 31/12/2010

	€	€
Sales		72,400
Less Cost of Sales		
Opening Stock	1,800	
Purchases	39,500	
	41,300	
Less Closing Stock	1,900	39,400
Gross Profit		33,000
Less Expenses		
Wages	9,000	
Light and Heat	300	
Insurance	500	
Telephone	200	10,200
Net Profit		22,800

Looking Good Health Centre
Profit and Loss Account for the Year Ending 31/12/2010

	€	€	
Income			
Clients' Fees	6000 + 251,500 − 3,000 + 2,000	256,500	
Interest	2500	2,500	
Profit from Shop		22,800	
			281,800
Less Expenditure			
Light, Heat and Fuel	3200 + 700 − 400 + 300 − 300	3,500	
Contract Cleaning	400 + 2,900 − 500	2,800	
Supplies	−2,100 + 27,800 + 1,700	27,400	
Wages	90,150 − 9,000	81,150	
Insurance	6,300 − 500	5,800	
Laundry	3,600	3,600	
Telephone & Postage	1,900 − 400	1,500	
Interest	**Note 4**	2,000	
Depreciation:	Buildings **Note 1**	18,000	
	Equipment **Note 2**	19,600	
	Furniture **Note 3**	6,000	
			171,350
Net Profit			110,450
Plus Reserves 1/1/2010			261,400
Profit and Loss 31/12/2010			371,850

Note 1.	Buildings	850,000	(34,000)	
	Extension	50,000		
	× 2%	900,000	(18,000)	
	Revaluation	50,000	52,000	102,000
		950,000	—	
Note 2.	Equipment	80,000	(32,000)	
	Addition	18,000		
	× 20%	98,000	(19,600)	
			(51,600)	
Note 3.	Furniture	30,000	(12,000)	
	× 20%		(6,000)	
		30,000	(18,000)	
Note 4.	Loan Amount Repaid		76,000	
	Loan Amount Borrowed		70,000	
	Interest for 18 Months		6,000	
	Interest for 6 Months (P&L)		2,000	
	Interest for 12 Months' Reserves 1/1		4,000	

Looking Good Health Centre
Balance Sheet as at 31/12/2010

	Cost €	Depreciation €	Net €
Fixed Assets			
Buildings and Grounds	950,000	–	950,000
Equipment	98,000	51,600	46,400
Furniture	30,000	18,000	12,000
	1,078,000	69,600	1,008,400
Investments			100,000
			1,108,400
Current Assets			
Bank	15,650		
Stock: Health Shop	1,900		
Heating Oil	400		
Cleaning Prepaid	500		
Clients' Fees Due	2,000		
		20,450	
Less Creditors: Amounts Falling Due within One Year			
Electricity Due	300		
Clients' Fees Prepaid	3,000		
Creditors for Supplies	1,700		
		5,000	
			15,450
Net Current Assets			1,123,850
Financed by			
	Auth.	Issued	
Share Capital and Reserves			
Ordinary Shares	950,000	650,000	650,000
Revaluation Reserve Note 1			102,000
Profit and Loss Balance			371,850
			1,123,850

Question 5.2

Included in the assets and liabilities of the Slimline Health Centre Ltd on 1/1/2010 were the following: buildings and grounds at cost €520,000; equipment at cost €90,000; furniture at cost €25,000; stock of health food for sale €1,500; heating oil €1,660; contract cleaning prepaid €300; creditors for supplies to health centre €1,450; clients' fees paid in advance €5,500, investments €80,000; authorised capital €450,000; issued capital €320,000. All fixed assets have three years' accumulated depreciation on 1/1/2010.

Receipts and Payments Account of Slimline Health Centre Ltd for the Year Ended 31/12/2010

Receipts	€	Payments	€
Current a/c Balance	7,560	Wages and Salaries	88,240
Clients' Fees	262,600	Insurance	6,300
Interest	2,160	Light and Heat	2,900
Shop Receipts	67,000	Purchases – Shop	41,300
Balance	9,500	Purchases – Supplies	38,600
		Laundry	4,100
		New Extension 1/1/2010	80,000
		Contract Cleaning	2,700
		Telephone and Postage	1,880
		Equipment	16,000
		Repayment of €60,000 Loan on 1/6/2010 with 17 Months' Interest	66,800
	€348,820		€348,820

You are given the following additional information and instructions:

1. Closing stock at 31/12/2010: shop €1,800; heating oil €360; electricity due 31/12/2010 €290.
2. Cleaning is done by contract payable monthly in advance and includes a payment of €400 for January 2011.
3. Clients' fees include fees for 2011 of €4,000.
4. Clients' fees in arrears at 31/12/2010 €650.
5. Wages and salaries include €16,000 per annum paid to the receptionist who also runs the shop. It is estimated that 60 per cent of this salary and €220 of the light and heat, €600 of the insurance and €360 of the telephone is attributable to the shop.
6. Slimline Health Centre Ltd decided to revalue buildings and grounds at €700,000 on 31/12/2010.
7. Depreciation to be provided as follows:
   Buildings – two per cent of cost for a full year.
   Equipment – 20 per cent of cost per annum.
   Furniture – 20 per cent of cost per annum.
8. Creditors for supplies to health centre at 31/12/2010 €1,600.

You are required to:

(a) Calculate the company's reserves on 1/1/2010. `20`

(b) Calculate the profit/loss from the health shop for the year ended 31/12/2010. `12`

(c) Prepare a profit and loss account for the year ended 31/12/2010. `36`

(d) Prepare a balance sheet on 31/12/2010. `32`

`100 marks`

Solution to Question 5.2

`20`

(a) Statement of Capital and Reserves on 1/1/2010

Assets		€	€
Buildings and Grounds	(520,000 – 31,200)	488,800 ❷	
Equipment	(90,000 – 54,000)	36,000 ❷	
Furniture	(25,000 – 15,000)	10,000 ❷	
Investment		80,000 ❶	
Stock – Health Food for Resale		1,500 ❶	
Stock – Oil		660 ❶	
Contract Cleaning Prepaid		300 ❶	
Cash at Bank		7,560 ❶	624,820
Less Liabilities			
Creditors for Supplies		1,450 ❶	
Customers' Advance Deposits		5,500 ❶	
Loan		60,000 ❷	
Interest on Loan (12 months @ €400 per month)		4,800 ❷	
Issued Capital		320,000 ❶	391,750
Reserves			233,070 ❷

`12`

(b) Health Shop Profit and Loss Account for Year Ended 31/12/2010

		€	€
Shop Receipts – Sales			67,000 ❷
Less Expenses			
Cost of Goods Sold	(1,500 + 41,300 – 1,800)	41,000 ❺	
Light and Heat		220 ❶	
Insurance		600 ❶	
Telephone		360 ❶	
Wages and Salaries	(60% of 16,000)	9,600 ❷	51,780
Contribution from Health Shop			15,220

36

(c) Profit and Loss Account for Year Ended 31/12/2010

Income		Workings	€	€
Interest Received			2,160 ❶	
Profit on Health Shop			15,220 ❶	
Customers' Fees		W1	264,750 ❹	282,130
Less Expenses				
Wages and Salaries	(88,240 – 9,600)		78,640 ❷	
Insurance	(6,300 – 600)		5,700 ❶	
Light and Heat		W2	3,270 ❺	
Purchases – Supplies		W3	38,750 ❸	
Loan Interest		W4	2,000 ❸	
Laundry			4,100 ❶	
Postage and Telephone			1,520 ❶	
Depreciation – Buildings		W5	12,000 ❶	
– Equipment			21,200 ❶	
– Furniture			5,000 ❶	
Contract Cleaning		W6	2,600 ❸	174,780
Net Profit for Year				107,350 ❼
Add Reserve 1/1/2010				233,070 ❶
Profit and Loss Balance 31/12/2010				340,420

36

(d) Balance Sheet as at 31/12/2010

Fixed Asset		Cost €	Depreciation €	Net €
Buildings and Grounds		700,000 ❶		700,000
Equipment	(90,000 + 16,000)	106,000 ❷	75,200 ❷	30,800
Furniture		25,000 ❷	20,000 ❷	5,000
		692,000	107,600	735,800
Investments				80,000 ❷
				815,800
Current Assets				
Closing Stock – Shop Goods		1,800 ❷		
– Oil		360 ❷		
Cleaning Prepaid		400 ❷		
Customers' Fees Due		650 ❷	3,210	

Less Creditors: Amounts Falling Due within One Year

Bank Overdraft	9,500 ❷		
Electricity Due	290 ❷		
Customers' Advance Deposits	4,000 ❷		
Creditors for Supplies	1,600 ❷	(15,390)	(12,180)
			803,620

Financed by

Share Capital and Reserves	Authorised	Issued	
Ordinary Shares	450,000 ❶	320,000 ❶	
Revaluation Reserve	W7	143,200 ❸	
Profit and Loss Balance		340,420	803,620
			803,620

Workings

1. **Customers' Fees** – Amount Received		262,600	
Add Advance Deposits		5,500	
Add Fees Due		650	
Less Fees Prepaid 31/12/2010		(4,000)	264,750
2. **Light and Heat** – Amount Paid		2,900	
Add Stock – Heating Oil 1/1/2010		660	
Add Electricity Due 31/12/2010		290	
Less Stock – Heating Oil 1/1/2010		(360)	
Less Charge to Shop		(220)	3,270
3. **Purchases** (38,600 + 1,600 − 1,450)			38,750
4. **Loan Interest** – Paid		6,800	
Less Interest Due 1/1/2010 for 1 year @ €400 per month		4,800	2,000
5. **Depreciation** – Buildings and Grounds 2%			12,000
× (520,000 + 80,000)			
– Equipment 20% × (90,000 + 16,000)		21,200	
– Furniture 20% × (25,000)		5,000	
6. **Contract Cleaning** – Amount Paid		2,700	
Add Amount Prepaid 1/1/2010		300	
Less Amount 31/12/2010		(400)	2,600
7. **Revaluation Reserve**			
Buildings (700,000 − 600,000 including extension)		100,000	
Depreciation (31,200 + 12,000)		43,200	143,200

Question 5.3

The following were included in the assets and liabilities of the Longlife Health Centre Ltd on 1/1/2010: buildings €600,000, equipment €80,000, furniture at cost €20,000, stock of health food €2,100, heating oil €540, creditors for supplies to health centre €1,350, six per cent investments 60,000, authorised capital €500,000, issued capital €350,000. All fixed assets have three years' accumulated depreciation on 1/1/2010.

Receipts and Payments a/c of the Longlife Health Centre Ltd for the Year Ended 31/12/2010

Receipts	€	Payments	€
Current a/c Balance	8,200	Insurance	5,900
Investment Income	2,400	Cleaning	3,200
Clients' Fees	260,500	Wages and Salaries	79,840
Shop Receipts	66,000	Light and Heat	3,100
		New extension	90,000
		Purchases – Shop	44,600
		Purchases – Supplies	35,400
		Equipment	15,000
		Telephone	1,800
		Repayment of €40,000 Loan on 1/7/2009 with 18 Months' Interest	45,400
		Balance	12,860
	337,100		337,100

You are given the following information and instructions:

1. Closing stocks at 31/12/10: shop €1,800, heating oil €340.
2. Clients' fees include fees for 2011 of € 3,600. Fees due at 31/12/10 €500.
3. Cleaning is done by contract and includes a payment of €400 for January 2010.
4. Wages and salaries include €22,000 per annum paid to the receptionist who also runs the shop. It is estimated that 40 per cent of this salary and €250 of the light and heat, €700 of the insurance and €400 of the telephone is attributable to the shop.
5. Creditors for supplies to the health centre at 31/12/2010 €1,900.
6. Depreciation to be provided as follows:
   Buildings – 2% of cost for a full year.
   Equipment – 20% of cost per annum
   Furniture – 20% of cost per annum.
7. Electricity due at 31/12/2010 €340.

You are required to:

(a) Calculate the company's reserves at 1/1/2010.
(b) Calculate the profit/loss from the health shop for the year ended 31/12/2010.

(c) Prepare a profit and loss account for the year ended 31/1/2010.

(d) Prepare a balance sheet at 31/12/2010.

Solution to Question 5.3

(a) Statement of Reserves at 1/1/2010

	Workings	Dr €	Cr €
Buildings	W1	600,000	
Accumulated Depreciation – Buildings			36,000
Equipment	W2	80,000	
Accumulated Depreciation – Equipment			48,000
Furniture	W3	20,000	
Accumulated Depreciation – Furniture			12,000
Stock: Health Food		2,100	
Heating Oil		540	
Creditors for Supplies			1,350
6% Investments		60,000	
Share Capital (Authorised €500,000)			350,000
Bank		8,200	
Loan			40,000
Interest			3,600
Reserves 1/1/2010			279,890
		770,840	770,840

(b) Shop Trading and Profit and Loss Account for the Year Ended 31/12/2010

	€	€
Sales		66,000
Less Cost of Sales		
Opening Stock	2,100	
Purchases	44,600	
Less Closing Stock	1,800	44,900
Gross Profit		21,100
Less Expenses		
Wages	8,800	
Light and Heat	250	
Insurance	700	
Telephone	400	10,150
Contribution from Shop	10,950	

(c) Profit and Loss Account for the Year Ended 31/12/2010

	€	€
Income		
Investment Interest	3,600	
Profit from Shop	10,950	
Fees 260,500 – 3,600 + 500	257,400	271,950
Less Expenditure		
Light and Heat 540 + 3,100 – 340 – 250 + 340	3,390	
Supplies 35,400 – 1,350 + 1,900	35,950	
Insurance 5,900 – 700	5,200	
Cleaning 3,200 – 400	2,800	
Wages and Salaries 79,840 – 8,800	71,040	
Telephone 1,800 – 400	1,400	
Interest	1,800	
Depreciation – Buildings	13,800	
– Equipment	19,000	
– Furniture	4,000	158,380
Net Profit	113,570	
+ Reserves 1/1	279,890	
Balance 31/12	393,460	

(d) Balance Sheet as at 31/12/2010

Fixed Asset	Cost €	Depreciation €	Net €
Buildings	690,000	49,800	640,200
Equipment	95,000	67,000	28,000
Furniture	20,000	16,000	4,000
	805,000	132,800	672,200
6% Investments			60,000
			732,200
Current Assets			
Investment Interest Due	1,200		
Bank	12,860		
Stocks: Health Shop	1,800		
Heating Oil	340		
Fees Due	500		
Cleaning Prepaid	400		
	17,100		

Less Creditors: Amounts Falling Due within 1 Year			
Fees in Advance	3,600		
Creditors for Supplies	1,900		
Electricity Due	340	5,840	11,260
			743,460

Financed by: Share Capital and Reserves	Authorised	Issued
Share Capital	500,000	350,000
Profit and Loss balance	393,460	743,460

Workings

1. Buildings		600,000	36,000
Extension		90,000	
× 2%		690,000	13,800
			49,800
B/S 600,000 × 2% × 3 = 36,000			
2. Equipment		80,000	48,000
		15,000	
× 20%		95,000	19,000
			67,000
3. Furniture		20,000	12,000
			4,000
			16,000
4. Investment Income 60,000 × 6% = 3,600 for year			
Received		2,400	
Due 31/12		1,200	
5. Loan Amount Repaid		45,400	
Amount Borrowed		40,000	
18 months' Interest		5,400	
1 month's Interest		300	
Year's Interest		3,600	

6 > Correction of Errors and Suspense Accounts

aims

- To be able to deal with **errors and omissions** in accounts using journal entries.
- To be able to transfer these to the suspense account, profit and loss account and balance sheet, thus **correcting** them.

exam focus

Correction of errors and suspense accounts are together regarded as the most difficult topic on the course. A good knowledge of **basic bookkeeping** is essential. All the questions require very **careful reading** and should never be rushed. You should use T accounts to record what **actually** happened and what **should have** been entered, and you should then compare this to what has been entered.

The real key to success with these questions is plenty of practice, but the following basic hints will be helpful.

1. When doing the journal entries, never just enter a single entry. **Always complete the double entry**.
2. Always write the **narration** under each entry.
3. As you go down through the journal entries, indicate beside each whether it is to go into the profit and loss account or the balance sheet.
4. In writing up the suspense account, simply **follow your own instructions**, i.e. where you indicated debit in the journal entry, do the same in the suspense and likewise with the credits.
5. In amending the balance sheet, debits on assets will be pluses, debits on liabilities minuses and vice versa with credits. Where you have, for example, a debit with a person's name, determine whether you are increasing a debtor or decreasing a creditor.

key point

In amending the profit and loss account, the debit items in the journal will be minuses and the credit items will be pluses.

Question 6.1

The trial balance of J. Nolan, a clothes shop owner, failed to agree, and the difference was placed in the suspense account. The following balance sheet was then prepared.

Balance Sheet at 31 December 2010

	(€)	(€)	(€)
Fixed Assets			
Premises		80,000	
Furniture and Equipment		60,000	140,000
Current Assets			
Stock (Including Suspense)		35,000	
Debtors		12,000	
		47,000	
Less Current Liabilities			
Creditors	15,000		
Bank	7,000	22,000	
Net Current Assets			25,000
			165,000
Financed by			
Capital	125,000		
Plus Net Profit	60,000		
	185,000		
Less Drawings	20,000	165,000	

When the books were checked, the following errors were discovered:

1. A private debt of €1,200 owed to Nolan had been offset in full against a business debt of €1,400 owed by Nolan.

2. Furniture sold on credit to P. Dolan for €2,760 had been entered in both the sales account and the wrong side of Dolan's account as €2,670.

3. A credit note received from a creditor for €456 had been entered in the purchases returns account as €465 and on the wrong side of the creditor's account as €546.

4. Goods previously sold to a debtor for €760 had been returned and entered in the books as €670. Subsequently Nolan decided to apply a restocking charge of 10 per cent of this amount, and credited the debtor with €603. No other entry had been made in the books in respect of the restocking charge.

5. Payments from the business bank account of €300 for private repairs and €250 for equipment repairs had been credited to creditors and equipment, respectively.

You are required to:

(a) Journalise the necessary corrections.

(b) Show the suspense account.

(c) Prepare a statement showing the correct net profit.

(d) Prepare the corrected balance sheet.

Solution to Question 6.1

(a) J. Nolan

	Entry	Debit (€)	Credit (€)
Creditor (i)	b	1,400	
Capital	b		1,200
Discount Received	p		200

Private debt used to offset business debt of €1,400.

	Entry	Dr (€)	Cr (€)
Sales (ii)	p	2,670	
P. Dolan (Debtor)	b	5,430	
Furniture	b		2,760
Suspense			5,340

Disposal of furniture entered as sales and on wrong side of Dolan's account.

	Entry	Dr (€)	Cr (€)
Creditors (iii)	b	1,002	
Purchases Returns	p	9	
Suspense			1,011

Wrong figure for credit note entered in accounts.

	Entry	Dr (€)	Cr (€)
Debtor (iv)	b	589	
Sales Returns	p	14	
Suspense			603

	Entry	Dr (€)	Cr (€)
Drawings (v)	b	300	
Equipment Repairs	p	250	
Creditors	b	300	
Equipment	b	250	
Suspense			1,100

(b) Suspense Account

	(€)		(€)
Difference	8,054	(ii) Sales, etc.	5,340
		(iii) Creditors, etc.	1,011
		(iv) Debtors, etc.	603
		(v) Drawings, etc.	1,100
	8,054		8,054

(c) Amended Net Profit

	Minus (€)	Plus (€)	(€)
Net Profit per Accounts			60,000
Discount Received		200	
Sales	(2,670)		
Purchases Returns	(9)		
Sales Returns	(14)		
Repairs	(250)		
	(2,943)	200	(2,743)
Corrected Profit			57,257

(d) Corrected Balance Sheet

	(€)	(€)
Fixed Assets		
Premises	80,000	
Furniture and Equipment (60,000 − 2,760 + 250)	57,490	
		137,490
Current Assets		
Stock (35,000 − 8,054)	26,946	
Debtors (12,000 + 5,430 + 589)	18,019	
	44,965	
Less Current Liabilities		
Creditors (15,000 − 1,400 − 1,000 − 300)	12,298	
Bank	7,000	19,298
Working Capital		25,667
		€163,157

Financed by	
Capital (125,000 + 1,200)	126,200
Add Net Profit	57,257
	183,457
Less Drawings (20,000 + 300)	(20,300)
	163,157

Question 6.2

The trial balance of R. Gillen, a grocer, failed to agree on 31 December 2010. The difference was entered in the suspense account, and the following balance sheet was prepared.

Balance Sheet at 31 December 2010

	(€)	(€)	(€)
Fixed Assets			
Premises		165,000	
Fixtures and Equipment		33,000	198,000
Current Assets			
Stock		94,000	
Debtors		10,600	
Cash		400	
		105,000	
Less Current Liabilities			
Creditors (Incorporating Suspense)	72,000		
Bank	19,000	91,000	14,000
			212,000
Financed by			
Capital		176,000	
Add Net Profit		42,000	
		218,000	
Less Drawings		6,000	212,000
			212,000

On checking the books, the following errors were revealed:

1. Gillen sent a cheque for €520 in full settlement of a business debt of €560, and this was recorded correctly in the books. However, no entry has been made in the books of the subsequent dishonouring of this cheque and the payment on account of €300 cash by Gillen.

2. Repairs to premises €600 and repairs to private dwelling house €360 were paid out of the business bank account and credited to premises account.

3. A private debt of €390 owed by Gillen to a debtor of the business had been offset in full settlement against a business debt of €400 owed to Gillen. No entry had been made in the books.

4. Gillen had given a private car, valued at €4,500, to a creditor of the business to offset, in full, a debt of €4,700. This transaction had been treated in error as a credit purchase of stock for €4,500.

5. Goods previously sold to a debtor for €530 had been returned to Gillen and entered in the books in error as €350. Subsequently, Gillen decided to apply a restocking charge of 10 per cent to these returns, and he immediately credited the debtor with €315. No other entry was made in the books in respect of the restocking charge.

You are required to:

(a) Journalise the necessary corrections.

(b) Show the suspense account.

(c) Prepare a statement showing the correct net profit.

(d) Prepare the corrected balance sheet.

Solution to Question 6.2

(a) R. Gillen

	Dr (€)	Cr (€)
Bank Account	520	
Discount	40	
Creditors Account		260
Cash		300

Being the recording of a dishonoured cheque issued by Gillen and payment on account of €300 in cash.

	Dr (€)	Cr (€)
Drawings/Capital Account	390	
Discount Account	10	
Debtors Account		400

Being a private debt of €400 owed by Gillen offset against a business debt of €530 owed to Gillen.

	Dr (€)	Cr (€)
Premises Account	960	
Drawings Account	360	
Repairs Account	600	
Suspense Account		1,920

Being cancellation of entry in premises account and recording of payments in drawings and repairs accounts.

	Dr (€)	Cr (€)
Creditors Account	9,200	
Purchase Account		4,500
Discount Received Account		200
Capital Account		4,500

Being recording of €4,500 introduced as capital by Gillen and cancellation of incorrect entries in creditors and purchases accounts.

	Dr (€)	Cr (€)
Debtors Account	188	
Sales Returns Account	127	
Suspense Account		315

Being the recording of restock charge and correction of incorrect entry in sales returns and debtors accounts.

(b) Suspense Account

(€)			(€)
Difference	2,235	Premises	960
		Drawings	360
		Repairs	600
		Debtors	315
	2,235		2,235

(c) Statement of Corrected Net Profit

	(€)	(€)
Net Profit as per Books		4,200
Add Purchases	4,500	
Discount Received	200	
		4,700
		46,700
Deduct Discount	40	
Repairs	600	
Discount	10	
Sales Returns	127	777
		45,923

(d) Corrected Balance Sheet at 31 December 2010

	(€)	(€)	(€)
Fixed Assets			
Premises		165,960	
Fixtures and Equipment		33,000	198,960
Current Assets			
Stock		94,000	
Debtors		10,388	
Cash		100	
		104,488	
Less Current Liabilities			
Creditors	65,295		
Bank	18,480	83,775	20,713
			219,673
Financed by			
Capital		180,500	
Add Net Profit		45,923	
		226,423	
Less Drawings	6,750	219,673	
			219,673

Question 6.3

The trial balance of P. Morgan, a garage owner, failed to agree on 31/12/2010. The difference was placed in a suspense account and the following balance sheet was prepared:

Balance Sheet as at 31/12/2010

	(€)	(€)	(€)
Fixed Assets			
Premises		250,000	
Equipment		72,000	322,000
Current Assets			
Stock (Including Suspense)		86,000	
Debtors		36,000	
		122,000	
Less Creditors: Amounts Falling Due within One Year			
Creditors	54,000		
Bank	29,000	83,000	39,000
			361,000
Financed by			
Capital		320,000	
Add: Net Profit		56,000	
		376,000	
Less: Drawings		15,000	361,000

On checking the books, the following errors were discovered:

1. A motor car purchased on credit from P. Bourke for €13,000 had been entered on the incorrect side of Bourke's account and credited as €1,300 in the equipment account.

2. A private debt of €1,470 owed by Morgan had been offset in full against a business debt of €1,500 owed to the firm for car repairs previously carried out. No entry had been made in the books in respect of this offset.

3. Morgan had won a private holiday for two worth €9,000 in total. One ticket had been given to a salesperson as part payment of sales commission for the year, and the other to an advertising firm as payment in full of a debt of €4,750. No entry had been made in the books.

4. Morgan had returned a motor car previously purchased on credit from a supplier for €13,400 and had entered this transaction in the relevant ledger accounts as €14,300. However, a credit note subsequently arrived from the supplier in respect of the return showing a transport charge of €300 to cover the cost of the return. The only entry in respect of this credit note was a credit in the creditors account of €13,100.

5. Car parts previously sold on credit for €350 were returned to Morgan. These goods had been incorrectly entered as €35 on the credit of the equipment account and as €53 on the debit of the purchases account.

You are required to:

(a) Journalise the necessary corrections.

(b) Show the suspense account.

(c) Prepare a statement showing the correct net profit.

(d) Prepare a corrected balance sheet.

Solution to Question 6.3

(a) P. Morgan, Garage Owner

Corrections	Dr €	Cr €
(i) Purchases	13,000	
Creditors		26,000
Equipment	1,300	
Suspense	11,700	
Purchase of car incorrectly recorded.		
(ii) Drawings	1,470	
Debtors		1,500
Discount Allowed	30	
Offset of private debt against business debt.		
(iii) Capital		9,000
Sales Commission	4,500	
Creditors	4,750	
Discount Received		250
Capital introduced in prizes used in business.		
(iv) Purchases Returns	1,200	
Creditors	11,900	
Suspense		13,100
Incorrect recording of credit and returns.		
(v) Sales Returns	350	
Debtors		350
Equipment	35	
Purchases		53
Suspense	18	
Car parts incorrectly entered.		

(b) Suspense Account

(i) Equipment	11,700	(iv) Creditors		13,100
(v) Purchases	18			
Difference	1,382			
	13,100			13,100

(c) Statement of Corrected Net Profit

			€
Net Profit per Accounts			56,000
Purchases	13,000		
Discount Allowed	30		
Sales Commission	4,500		
Discount Received		250	
Purchases Returns	1,200		
Sales Returns	350		
Purchases		53	
	19,080	303	18,777
Corrected Profit			37,223

(d) Corrected Balance Sheet

		€	€	€
Fixed Assets				
Premises	250,000		250,000	
Equipment	72,000 + 1,300 + 35		73,335	
				323,335
Current Assets				
Stock	86,000 − 1,382	84,618		
Debtors	36,000 − 1,500 − 350	34,150		
			118,768	
Creditors: Amounts Falling Due within One Year				
Creditors	54,000 + 26,000 − 4,750 − 11,900	63,350		
Bank	29,000	29,000		
			92,350	
Net Current Assets				26,418
				349,753
Financed by				
Capital	320,000 + 9,000		329,000	
Plus Correct Profit			37,223	
			366,223	
Less Drawings	15,000 + 1,470		16,470	
				349,753

Question 6.4

The trial balance of S. Craddock, a furniture and carpet trader, failed to agree on 31/12/2010. The difference was entered in a suspense account and the following balance sheet was prepared.

Balance Sheet as at 31/12/2010

	€	€
Fixed Assets		
Premises	650,000	
Fixtures and Fittings	72,000	722,000
Current Assets		
Stock (Including Suspense)	88,600	
Debtors	33,300	
Cash	400	
	122,300	
Less: Current Liabilities		
Creditors	52,000	
Bank	27,000	79,000	43,300
			765,300
Financed by:		
Capital	730,000	
Add: Net Profit	63,300	
	793,300	
Less: Drawings	28,000	765,300
		765,300

On checking the books, the following errors were discovered:

1. Furniture, purchased on credit from J. Dolan for €16,500, had been entered as €6,500 on the incorrect side of Dolan's account and credited as €1,650 in the fixtures and fittings account.

2. A debtor who owed Craddock €900 sent a cheque for €750 and €100 in cash in full settlement. This was correctly recorded in the books. However, no entry had been made in the books of the subsequent dishonouring of this cheque or of the writing-off of the remaining debt in full because of bankruptcy.

3. Bedside lockers previously sold on credit for €340 had been returned to Craddock. These goods had been incorrectly entered as €34 on the credit of the fixtures and fittings account and as €40 on the debit of the purchases account.

4. A private debt for €1,600, owed by Craddock, had been offset in full against a business debt of €1,700, owed to the firm for carpet repairs previously carried out. No entry had been made in the books in respect of this offset.

5. Craddock had returned furniture, previously purchased on credit from a supplier for €8,800, and had entered this transaction in the relevant ledger accounts incorrectly as €8,880. However, a credit note subsequently arrived from the supplier in respect of the return showing a transport charge of €200 to cover the cost of the return. The only entry made in respect to this credit note was a credit of €8,600 in the creditors account.

You are required to:

(a) Journalise the necessary corrections. `55`

(b) Show the suspense account. `10`

(c) Prepare a statement showing the correct net profit. `15`

(d) Prepare a corrected balance sheet. `20`

`100 marks`

Solution to Question 6.4

`55`

(a) Journal Entries

	Dr €	Cr €
1. Fixture and Fittings	1,650 ❸	
Purchases	16,500 ❸	
Creditors/Dolan		23,000 ❸
Suspense	4,850 ❸	
Being correction of incorrect recording of the purchase of furniture on credit.		
2. Debtor Account	800 ❷	
Bank Account		750 ❷
Discount Allowed Disallowed		50 ❸
Bad Debts Account	800 ❸	
Debtor		800 ❷
Being recording of dishonouring a cheque and recording of a bad debt.		
3. Fixtures and Fittings	34 ❸	
Purchases		40 ❸
Suspense	6 ❸	
Sales Returns	340 ❷	
Debtors		340 ❷
Being lockers returned by a customer entered incorrectly in the books.		

4.	Drawings			1,600 ❸	
	Discount Allowed			100 ❸	
	Debtors				1,700 ❸
	Being recording of an offset of a private debt owed by Craddock against a debt owed by a customer to the firm.				
5.	Creditors			8,320 ❸	
	Suspense				8,600 ❸
	Purchases Returns			280 ❸	
	Being correction of incorrect recording of a credit note and recording of a charge for returns				

penalty of 5 × 1 mark for each narrative omitted

(b) Suspense Account   `10`

		€			€
Purchases	(i)	4,850 ❸			
Purchases	(ii)	6 ❸			
*Original Difference		3,744 ❶	Creditors (v)		8,600 ❸
		8,600			8,600

*Originally included in stock. The stock figure is now €88,600 − €3,744 = €84,856

(c) Statement of Correct Net Profit   `15`

		€	€
Original Net Profit as per Books			63,300 ❶
Add Discount Disallowed			50 ❷
Purchases			40 ❷
			63,390
Less Purchases		16,500 ❶	
Bad Debts		800 ❶	
Sales Returns		340 ❶	
Discount Allowed		100 ❶	
Purchases Returns		280 ❷	18,020
Correct Net Profit			45,370 ❹

(d) Balance Sheet as at 31/12/2010 `20`

		€	€	€
Fixed Assets				
Premises				650,000 ❶
Fixtures and Fittings (72,000 + 1,650 + 34)				73,684 ❸
				723,684
Current Assets				
Stock	(88,600 − 3,744)		84,856 ❷	
Debtors	(33,300 − 1,700 − 340)		31,260 ❸	
Cash			400 ❶	
			116,516	
Less Creditors: Amounts Falling Due within One Year				
Creditors	(52,000 − 8,320 + 23,000)	66,680 ❸		
Bank	(27,000 + 750)	27,750 ❷	94,430	22,086
				745,770 ❶
Financed by				
Capital			730,000 ❶	
+ Net Profit			45,370	
			775,370	
− Drawings	(28,000 + 1,600)		29,600 ❷	745,770
				745,770 ❶

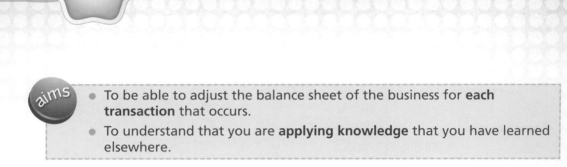

7 Tabular Statements

Question 7.1

The financial position of Macken Ltd on 1 January 2010 is shown in the following balance sheet.

Balance Sheet at 1 January 2010

	Cost (€)	Accumulated Depreciation (€)	Net (€)
Fixed Assets			
Land and Buildings	175,000		175,000
Motor Vehicles	69,000	29,000	40,000
	24,000	29,000	215,000
Current Assets			
Stock		56,000	
Debtors		39,000	
Insurance Prepaid		3,000	
		98,000	

Less Current Liabilities			
Creditors	46,000		
Bank Overdraft	24,000		
Expenses Due	1,500	71,500	26,500
			241,500
Financed by			
Share Capital			
Authorised: 250,000 Ordinary Shares @ €1 Each			
Issued: 160,000 Ordinary Shares @ €1 Each			160,000
Reserves			
Share Premium		40,000	
Profit and Loss		41,500	81,500
			241,500

The following transactions took place during 2010:

January: Macken Ltd purchased an adjoining business which included buildings €85,000; stock €34,000; creditors €25,000. The purchase price was discharged by granting the seller 60,000 shares in Macken Ltd at a premium of 30 cent and €25,000 by cheque.

February: The remaining shares were issued at a premium of 30 cent.

March: Sold goods on credit for €72,000, which is cost price plus 20 per cent.

April: Goods originally costing €500 were returned. Owing to their condition, a credit note for 20 per cent less than the selling price was issued.

May: €500 was received from a debtor previously written off as bad. This represented 25 per cent of the original amount, and the debtor has undertaken to pay the balance in September.

June: Paid a creditor a cheque for €600, having received a €730 discount.

September: Received balance of previously written-off debt as agreed in May.

October: Disposed of van for €9,000, which originally cost €17,000. The book value of the disposed van was €8,000. Acquired new van for €20,000. Depreciation for the year on all vehicles was €11,000.

November: Purchased goods from supplier for a total cost price of €10,000. Paid half by cheque less five per cent discount. The other half was on credit.

You are required to:

Record on a tabular statement the effects each of these transactions had on the relevant asset and liability and to ascertain the total assets and liabilities on 31 December 2010.

Solution to Question 7.1

Macken Ltd Tabular Statement

	(€)	Jan (€)	Feb (€)	Mar (€)	Apr (€)	May (€)	June (€)	Sept (€)	Oct (€)	Nov (€)	Total (€)
Assets											
Land and Buildings	175,000	85,000									260,000
Motor Vehicle	69,000								3,000		72,000
Depreciation	(29,000)								(2,000)		(31,000)
Stock	56,000	34,000		(60,000)	**W1** 480					10,000	40,480
Debtors	39,000			72,000	(480)	1,500		(1,500)			110,520
Insurance Prepaid	3,000										3,000
Goodwill		9,000									9,000
	313,000	128,000	0	12,000	0	1,500	0	(1,500)	1,000	10,000	464,000
Creditors	46,000	25,000					(630)			5,000	75,370
Bank	24,000	25,000	(39,000)			(500)	600	(1,500)	11,000	4,750	24,350
Expenses Due	1,500										1,500
Share Capital	160,000	60,000	30,000								250,000
Shared Return	40,000	18,000	9,000								67,000
Profit and Loss	41,500			12,000		2,000	30		(10,000)	250	45,780
	313,000	128,000	0	12,000	0	1,500	0	(1,500)	1,000	10,000	464,000

Working

W1

$$500 + 20\% = €600$$
$$7,600 - 20\% = €480$$
$$\text{Cost of Goods} = €500$$
$$\text{Value} = €480$$

Use €480 as lower price − condition of goods.

Question 7.2

The financial position of CMW Ltd on 1 January 2010 is shown in the following balance sheet:

Balance Sheet at 1 January 2010

	Cost (€)	Depreciation (€)	Net (€)
Fixed Assets			
Land and Buildings	150,000		150,000
Vehicles	88,000	18,000	70,000
Goodwill	50,000		50,000
	288,000	18,000	270,000
Current Assets			
Stock		60,000	
Debtors		44,000	
		104,000	
Current Liabilities			
Creditors	37,000		
Bank	19,000		
Expenses Due	600	56,600	47,400
			317,400
Financed by			
Capital			
Authorised: 330,000 @ €1			
Issued: 220,000 @ €1			220,000
Reserves			
Share Premium		45,000	
Profit and Loss Balance		52,400	97,400
			317,400

The following transactions took place during 2010:

January: Goods were sold on credit at a mark-up of 20 per cent for €6,000.

February: CMW Ltd purchased an adjoining business made up of buildings €65,000 and stock €15,000. The purchase price was discharged by granting the seller 70,000 shares at a premium of 20 cent per share.

April: Received a cheque for €400 from a debtor and allowed a discount of €20.

June: Delivery van originally costing €15,000 was traded against a new van costing €24,000. An allowance of €9,500 was made for the old van. Depreciation to date on the old van was €6,500, and the depreciation for the year was €15,000.

August: Paid by cheque a creditor's account of €800 and received a five per cent discount.

September: Received first and final dividend of €80 from a debtor who was declared bankrupt. This amounted to 40 cent in the euro.

November: Goods previously sold for €120 were returned. Because of the delay in returning the goods, a credit note for only €110 was issued.

December: Received €50,000 from issue of remaining shares.

You are required to:

Record on a tabular statement the effect each of these transactions had on the relevant asset and liability and to ascertain the total assets and liabilities on 31 December 2010.

Solution to Question 7.2

CMW Ltd Tabular Statement

	(€)	Jan (€)	Feb (€)	Apr (€)	Jun (€)	Aug (€)	Sept (€)	Nov (€)	Dec (€)	Total (€)
Assets										
Land and Buildings	150,000		65,000							215,000
Vehicles	88,000				9,000					97,000
Depreciation	(18,000)				(8,500)					(26,500)
Goodwill	50,000		4,000							54,000
Stock	60,000	(5,000)	15,000					100		70,100
Debtors	44,000	6,000		(420)			(200)	(110)		49,270
	374,000	1,000	84,000	(420)	500	0	(200)	(10)	0	458,870
Liabilities										
Bank	19,000			(400)	14,500	760	(80)		(50,000)	(16,220)
Creditors	37,000					(800)				36,200
Expenses Due	600									600
Share Capital	220,000		70,000						40,000	330,000
Share Premium	45,000		14,000						10,000	69,000
Profit and Loss	52,300	1,000		(20)	(14,000)	40	(120)	(10)		39,290
	374,000	1,000	84,000	(420)	500	0	200	(10)	0	458,870

Question 7.3

The financial position of Casey Ltd on 1/1/2010 is shown in the following balance sheet:

Balance Sheet as at 1/1/2010

	Cost (€)	Dep. to Date (€)	Net (€)
Fixed Assets			
Land and Buildings	460,000	13,800	446,200
Delivery Vans	76,000	33,000	43,000
	536,000	46,800	489,200
Current Assets			
Stock	59,800		
Insurance Prepaid	1,500		
Debtors	61,700	123,000	
Less Creditors: Amount Falling Due within One Year			
Creditors	62,500		
Bank	10,100		
Wages Due	2,400	75,000	
Net Current Assets			48,000
			537,200
Financed by			
Capital and Reserves			
Authorised – 850,000 Ordinary Shares @ €1 Each			
Issued – 430,000 Ordinary Shares @ €1 Each		430,000	
Share Premium		40,000	
Profit and Loss Balance		67,200	
		537,200	

The following transactions took place during 2010:

January: Casey Ltd decided to revalue the land and buildings at €580,000 on 1/1/2010, which includes land now valued at €100,000.

February: On 1/2/2010 Casey Ltd bought an adjoining business which included buildings €360,000, delivery vans €58,000, stock €25,000 and creditors €33,000. The purchase price was discharged by granting the seller 400,000 shares in Casey Ltd at a premium of 20c per share.

March: Goods previously sold by Casey Ltd for €1,800 were returned. The selling price of these goods was cost plus 20 per cent. Owing to the delay in returning these goods, a credit note was issued showing a deduction of 10 per cent of invoice price as a restocking charge.

April: A delivery van which cost €20,000 was traded in against a new van costing €36,000. An allowance of €12,500 was made for the old van. Depreciation to date on the old van was €6,600.

May: Received a bank statement on 31 May showing a direct debit of €4,800 to cover fire insurance for year ended 31/5/2011.

July: A payment of €720 was received from a debtor whose debt had been previously written off and who now wished to trade with Casey Ltd again. This represents 60 per cent of the original debt and the debtor had undertaken to pay the remainder of the debt in January 2011.

December: The buildings depreciation charge for the year to be two per cent of book value. The depreciation charge to be calculated from date of valuation and date of purchase. The total depreciation charge on delivery vans for the year was €22,000.

You are required to:

Record on a tabular statement the effect each of the above transactions had on the relevant asset and liability and ascertain the total assets and liabilities on 31/12/2010.

60 marks

Solution to Question 7.3

60

	1/1/2010 €	January €	February €	March €	April €	May €	July €	December €	Total €
Assets									
Land and Buildings	460,000	120,000 ②	360,000 ②						940,000
Accumulated Depreciation	(13,800)	13,800 ②						(16,200) ②	(16,200)
Delivery Vans	76,000		58,000 ②		16,000 ②				150,000
Accumulated Depreciation	(33,000)				6,600 ②			(22,000) ①	(48,400)
Stock	59,800		25,000 ②	1,500 ③					86,300
Debtors	61,700			(1,620) ②			480 ③		60,560
Insurance a/c (Prepaid)	1,500					4,800 ③		(4,300) ①	2,000 ①
Goodwill			70,000 ③						70,000
TOTAL	612,200	133,800	513,000	(120)	22,600	4,800	480	(42,500)	1,244,260 ①
Liabilities									
Share Capital	430,000		400,000 ②						830,000
Share Premium	40,000		80,000 ②						120,000
Revaluation Reserve		133,800 ③							133,800
Profit and Loss	67,200			(120) ①	(900) ③		1,200 ②	(42,500) ③	24,880 ②
Creditors	62,500		33,000 ②						95,500
Wages Due	2,400								2,400
Bank	10,100				23,500 ①	4,800 ②	(720) ①		37,680 ①
TOTAL	612,200	133,800	513,000	(120)	22,600	4,800	480	(42,500)	1,244,260 ①

Question 7.4

The financial position of Sadler Ltd on 1/1/2010 is shown in the following balance sheet:

Balance Sheet as at 1/1/2010

	Cost (€)	Dep. to Date (€)	Net (€)
Fixed Assets			
Land and Buildings	250,000	20,000	230,000
Equipment	40,000	15,000	25,000
	290,000	35,000	255,000
Current Assets			
Stock		65,000	
Debtors (Less Provision 5%)		76,000	
		141,000	
Less Creditors: Amount Falling Due within One Year			
Creditors	59,000		
Bank	21,000		
Expenses Due	2,000	82,000	
Net Current Assets			59,000
			314,000
Financed by:			
Capital and Reserves			
Authorised – 400,000 Ordinary Shares @ €1 Each			280,000
Issued – 280,000 Ordinary Shares @ €1 Each			12,000
Share Premium			22,000
Profit and Loss Balance			314,000

The following transactions took place during 2010:

January: Sadler Ltd bought an adjoining business which included buildings €110,000, debtors €15,000 and creditors €35,000. The purchase price was discharged by granting the seller 80,000 shares in Sadler Ltd at a premium of 25c per share.

February: Sadler Ltd decided to revalue the land and buildings at €500,000, which includes land valued at €50,000 on 28/2/2010.

March: A payment of €900 was received from a debtor whose debt had been previously written off and who now wished to trade with Sadler Ltd again. This represents 60 per cent of the original debt and the debtor had undertaken to pay the remainder of the debt by December 2010.

April: Goods previously sold for €720 were returned. The selling price of these goods was cost plus 20 per cent. Owing to the delay in returning these goods, a credit note was issued showing a deduction of 10 per cent of selling price as a restocking charge.

May: Received a bank statement on 31 May showing a direct debit of €1,800 to cover van insurance for year ended 31/3/2011 and a credit transfer received of €3,600 representing nine months' rent in advance from 1 May.

June: A creditor who was owed €400 by Sadler Ltd accepted equipment, the book value of which was €300, in full settlement of the debt. This equipment had cost €800.

July: An interim dividend of 6c per share was paid.

Oct: Received €50,000 from the issue of the remaining shares.

Nov: Received balance of previously written-off bad debt as agreed in March.

Dec: The buildings are to be depreciated at the rate of two per cent per annum of value at 28/2/2010.

You are required to:

Record on a tabular statement the effect each of the above transactions had on the relevant asset and liability and ascertain the total assets and liabilities on 31/12/2010.

100 marks

Solution to Question 7.4

100

	1/1/2010	Jan	Feb	Mar	Apr	May	Jun	Jul	Oct	Nov	Dec	31/12/2010
Land and Buildings	250,000	+10,000	+140,000									500,000
Depreciation	(20,000)	②	(−20,000) ③								(7,500)	(7,500)
Equipment	40,000		③				−800 ③				④	39,200
Depreciation	(15,000)				④		(−500) ③					(14,500)
Stock	65,000				+600 ④							65,600
Debtors	80,000	+15,000		+600 ③	(648) ④					(600) ③		94,352
Bad Debts Provision	(4,000)	②		③	④					③		(4,000)
Goodwill		+10,000 ②										10,000
Insurance a/c (Prepaid)						+1,800 ③					(1,350) ①	450 ②
	396,000	+135,000	+160,000	+600	(48)	+1,800	(300)			(600)	(8,850)	683,602
Ordinary Shares	280,000	+80,000							+40,000 ③	(600)		400,000
Share Premium	12,000	+20,000							+10,000 ③			42,000
Profit and Loss Balance	22,000			+1,500 ①	(48) ①		+100 ①	(21,600) ①			① (7,500) ① (1,350) ① 3,200	(3,698) ⑤
Creditors	59,000	+35,000 ③		(900) ③		(3,600) ③	(400) ③	+21,600 ③	(50,000)	(600) ②		93,600
Bank	21,000	③				+1,800 ③			②	②	(10,700) ②	(10,700) ②
Expenses Due	2,000		④							①		2,000
Revaluation Reserve			+160,000									160,000
Rent Receivable						+3,600	(300)				(3,200)	400 ②
	396,000	+135,000	+160,000	+600	(48)	+1,800	(300)			(600)	(8,850)	683,602

8 ▸ Depreciation and Revaluation

aims

- To be able to calculate the **different forms of depreciation**, showing all the relevant figures.
- To be able to deal with all increases in the value of fixed assets showing all the relevant **revaluation accounts** and all figures.

exam focus

Questions on both of these topics are popular in Section 1 of the examination. The key to success in both areas is to read through the questions carefully and to have a systematic approach.

Questions about depreciation and revaluation can sound complicated – but really they just need to be tackled in a logical way. Here's how:

1. With depreciation questions, it's vital that you show all your **calculations**, as most of the marks are allocated for these.

2. Determine immediately whether the depreciation is to be calculated from **cost price** or the **written-down value**.

3. Calculate carefully the total amount of depreciation written off from date of purchase to the beginning of the question for each fixed asset separately, **showing all your figures**.

4. With **mid-year acquisitions/disposals**, slowly count off on your fingers the number of months the asset was in the company's possession during the year in question.

To answer revaluation questions, consider the following:

1. This will involve land and buildings. Always remember that **land is not depreciated**. When land is revalued, this will simply mean an increase in the asset value.

2. When buildings are revalued, the asset value is increased to the relevant amount and the accumulated depreciation is **eliminated**.

3. Further depreciation on the buildings is usually calculated based on the **remaining useful life** of the buildings.

Question 8.1

Mooney Transport Ltd prepares its final accounts to 31 December each year. The company's policy is to depreciate its vehicles at the rate of 20 per cent of book value per annum calculated from date of purchase to date of disposal and to accumulate this depreciation in the provision for depreciation account.

On 1 January 2009 the company owned the following vehicles:

> Vehicle No. 1 purchased on 1 January 2005 for €35,000.
> Vehicle No. 2 purchased on 1 January 2006 for €40,000.
> Vehicle No. 3 purchased on 1 January 2007 for €44,000.

On 1 October 2009 vehicle No. 1 was traded against a new vehicle costing €50,000. Vehicle No. 1 had had a tachograph, which cost €6,000, fitted on 1 January 2007. The trade-in allowance was €15,000.

On 1 May 2010 vehicle No. 2 was crashed and traded against a new vehicle costing €55,000. The company received compensation of €12,000 and the cheque paid for the new vehicle was €43,000.

Show, with workings, to the nearest euro for 2009 and 2010:

(**a**) The vehicles account.

(**b**) The provision for depreciation account.

(**c**) The disposal account.

Solution to Question 8.1

(a) Vehicles Account

2009			(€)	2009		(€)
1 Jan	Balance B/D		125,000	1 Oct	Disposal	41,000
1 Oct	Trade-in	15,000				
	Bank	35,000	50,000	31 Dec	Balance C/D	134,000
			175,000			175,000
2010			**(€)**	**2010**		**(€)**
1 Jan	Balance B/D		134,000	1 May	Disposal	40,000
1 May	Trade-in	12,000				
	Bank	43,000	55,000	31 Dec	Balance C/D	149,000
			189,000			189,000

(b) Provision for Depreciation Account

2009		(€)	2009		(€)
1 Oct	Disposal	25,550	1 Jan	Balance B/D	58,184
31 Dec	Balance C/D	47,588	31 Dec	Profit and Loss	14,954
		73,138			73,138
2010		(€)	2010		(€)
1 May	Disposal	24,707	1 Jan	Balance B/D	47,588
31 Dec	Balance C/D	45,311	31 Dec	Profit and Loss	22,430
		70,018			70,018
			2005		
			1 Jan	Balance B/D	45,311

(c) Disposal Account

2009		(€)	2009		(€)
1 Oct	Vehicle 1 + Tachograph	41,000	1 Oct	Depreciation	25,550
				Trade-in	15,000
				Profit and Loss	450
		41,000			41,000
2010		(€)	2010		(€)
1 May	Vehicle	40,000	1 May	Depreciation	24,706
	Profit and Loss	8,706		Trade-in	12,000
				Insurance Company	12,000
		48,706			48,706

Workings

W1

Vehicle 1

	Cost/Net (€)	Depreciation (€)	Net (€)
2005	35,000	7,000	28,000
2006	28,000	5,600	22,400
2007	22,400	4,480	17,920
2008	17,920	3,584	14,336
		(i) 20,664	
2009	(iii) 14,336 × 20% × 0.75	2,150	
		(ii) 22,814	

W2

Vehicle 2

	Cost/Net (€)	Depreciation (€)	Net (€)
2006	40,000	8,000	32,000
2007	32,000	6,400	25,600
2008	25,600	5,120	20,480
		(i) 19,520	
2009	(iii) 20,480	4,096	
2010	(iv) $16,384 \times 20\% \times \frac{1}{3}$	1,091	
	Total to disposal		24,707

W3

Vehicle 3

	Cost/Net (€)	Depreciation (€)	Net (€)
2007	44,000	8,800	35,200
2008	35,200	7,040	28,160
		(i) 15,840	
2009	(iii) 28,160	5,632	
2010	(iv) 22,528	4,506	

W4

Tachograph

	Cost/Net (€)	Depreciation (€)	Net (€)
2007	6,000	1,200	4,800
2008	4,800	960	
		(i) 2,160	
2009	(iii) 3840 × 20% × $\frac{3}{4}$	576	
		(ii) 2,736	

W5

Vehicle 4

	Cost/Net (€)	Depreciation (€)	Net (€)
2009	(iii) 50,000		2,500
2010	(iv) 47,500	9,500	

W6

Vehicle 5

	Cost/Net (€)	Depreciation (€)	Net (€)
2010	(iv) 55,000 × 20% × $\frac{2}{3}$	7,333	

(i) Depreciation to 2009	(ii) Depreciation Disposal 1	(iii) Depreciation 2009	(iv) Depreciation 2010
20,664	22,814	2,150	1,091
19,520	2,736	4,096	4,506
15,840		5,632	9,500
2,160	25,550	576	7,333
		2,500	
58,184			22,430
		14,954	

Question 8.2

High 'n' Mighty Plc purchased property on 1 January 2000 consisting of land €150,000 and buildings €340,000. The estimated useful life of the buildings was 50 years with a nil residual value at the end of the period. Depreciation is provided on a straight-line basis.

On 1 January 2010 the property was revalued to €960,000. Of this revaluation €300,000 was attributed to the land. (Land is not depreciated.) The remaining useful life of the buildings at the date of revaluation is to be left unchanged at 40 years.

Show:
(a) (i) Land and buildings account.

  (ii) Provision for depreciation account.

  (iii) Revaluation reserve account all for 2010.

(b) The relevant extracts from the final accounts relating to 2010.

Solution to Question 8.2

High 'n' Mighty Plc
(a) (i) Land and Buildings Accounts

2010		(€)	2010		(€)
1 Jan	Balance B/D	490,000	31 Dec	Balance C/D	960,000
1 Jan	Revaluation Reserve	470,000			
		960,000			960,000
2011		(€)			
1 Jan	Balance B/D	960,000			

(ii) Provision for Depreciation Account

2010		(€)	2010		(€)
1 Jan	Revaluation Reserve	68,000	1 Jan	Balance C/D	68,000
31 Dec	Balance C/D	16,500	31 Dec	Profit and Loss	16,500
		84,500			84,500
			2011		(€)
			1 Jan	Balance C/D	16,500

(iii) Revaluation Reserve Account

2009		(€)	2009		(€)
31 Dec	Balance C/D	438,000	1 Jan	Land and Buildings	470,000
			1 Jan	Provision for Depreciation	68,000
		438,000			438,000
			2008		**(€)**
			1 Jan	Balance C/D	438,000

(b) Balance Sheet at 31 December 2010

	(€)
Tangible Fixed Assets	
Land and Buildings	960,000
Less Depreciation	16,500
	943,000
Reserves	
Revaluation Reserve	438,000

Question 8.3

Moroney Ltd acquired property on 1 January 2001 consisting of land €200,000 and buildings €420,000. The estimated useful life of the buildings was 40 years with a nil residual value at the end of the period. Depreciation is provided for on a straight-line basis.

On 1 January 2010 the property was revalued at €870,000. Of this, €350,000 was attributable to the land. Land is not depreciated. The remaining useful life of the buildings at the date of revaluation is to be left unchanged.

Show:

(a) The land and buildings account.

(b) The revaluation reserve account.

(c) The provision for depreciation account.

Solution to Question 8.3

Moroney Ltd
(a) Land and Buildings Account

2010		(€)	2010		(€)
1 Jan	Balance B/D	620,000	31 Dec	Balance C/D	870,000
1 Jan	Revaluation Reserve	250,000			
		870,000			870,000
2011		**(€)**			
1 Jan	Balance B/D	870,000			

(b) Revaluation Reserve Account

2010		(€)	2010		(€)
31 Dec	Balance C/D	344,500	1 Jan	Provision for Depreciation	94,500
				Land and Buildings	250,000
		344,500			344,500
			2011		**(€)**
			1 Jan	Balance B/D	344,500

(c) Provision for Depreciation Account

2010		(€)	2010		(€)
1 Jan	Revaluation Reserve	94,500	1 Jan	Balance B/D	94,500
31 Dec	Balance C/D	16,744	31 Dec	Profit and Loss	16,744
		111,274			111,274
			2011		**(€)**
			1 Jan	Balance B/D	16,744

Question 8.4

Midwest Transport Ltd prepares its final accounts to 31 December each year. The company's policy is to depreciate its vehicles at the rate of 20 per cent of book value per annum calculated from the date of purchase to the date of disposal and to accumulate this depreciation in the provision for depreciation account.

On 1 January 2009 Midwest Transport Ltd owned the following vehicles:

Vehicle No. 1 purchased on 1 January 2006 for €40,000.
Vehicle No. 2 purchased on 1 January 2007 for €39,000.
Vehicle No. 3 purchased on 1 January 2008 for €42,000.

On 1 September 2009 Vehicle No. 1 was traded for €16,000 against a new vehicle costing €54,000. Vehicle No. 1 had had a tachograph fitted on 1 January 2007 costing €6,000. On 1 April 2010 Vehicle No. 3 was crashed and traded against a new vehicle costing €64,000. The company received compensation to the value of €8,000, and the cheque paid for the new vehicle was €53,000.

You are required to show, with workings, to the nearest €1, for each of the two years 2009 and 2010:

(a) The vehicles account.

(b) The provision for depreciation account.

(c) The vehicles disposal account.

Solution to Question 8.4

Midwest Transport Ltd
(a) Vehicle Account

2009		(€)	2009		(€)
1 Jan	Balance	127,000	1 Sept	Disposal	46,000
1 Sept	Bank	54,000	31 Dec	Balance	135,000
		181,000			181,000
2010		(€)	2010		(€)
1 Jan	Balance	135,000	1 Apr	Disposal	42,000
1 Apr	Bank	64,000	31 Dec	Balance	157,000
		199,000			199,000

(b) Provision for Depreciation Account

2009		Workings	(€)	2009		Workings	(€)
1 Sept	Disposal	W4	24,923	1 Jan	Balance	W1	44,120
31 Dec	Balance		37,752	31 Dec	Profit and Loss	W2	18,555
			62,675				62,675
2010		**Workings**	**(€)**	**2010**		**Workings**	**(€)**
1 Apr	Disposal	W5	16,464	1 Jan	Balance		37,752
31 Dec	Balance		46,306	31 Dec	Profit and Loss	W3	25,018
			62,770				62,770

(c) Disposal Account

2009		(€)	2009		(€)
1 Sept	Vehicle No. 1	46,000	1 Sept	Provision Account	24,923
				Allowance	16,000
			31 Dec	Profit and Loss	5,077
		€46,000			€46,000
2010		**(€)**	**2010**		**(€)**
1 Apr	Vehicle No. 3	42,000	1 Apr	Provision Account	16,464
				Compensation	8,000
				Allowance	11,000
			31 Dec	Profit and Loss	6,536
		42,000			42,000

Workings

W1
Depreciation Balance 1 January 2009

Vehicle No.	(€)	(€)
1	21,680	
2	14,040	
3	8,400	44,120

W2   Depreciation for 2009

Vehicle No.	(€)	(€)
1	3,243	
2	4,992	
3	6,720	
4	3,600	18,555

W3

Depreciation for 2010

Vehicle No.	(€)	(€)
2	3,994	
3	1,344	
4	10,080	
5	9,600	25,018

W4

Total Depreciation on Vehicle No. 1

Depreciation	(€)	(€)
To 1 January 2009	21,680	
For 2009	3,243	24,923

W5

Total Depreciation on Vehicle No. 3

Depreciation	(€)	(€)
To 1 January 2009	8,400	
For 2009	6,720	
For 2010	1,344	16,464

Question 8.5

On 1 January 2006 Quinn Ltd purchased buildings for €120,000. These buildings were expected to have a useful life of 50 years. During the year ended 31 December 2008, €38,000 was paid to a building contractor for an extension to the buildings. The company's own employees worked on the extension, and they were paid wages amounting to €10,000 by the company for this work. On 14 July 2009 the building was partially damaged by a storm, and the company spent €2,000 on repairs. On 1 January 2010 the building was valued by professional valuers at €230,000, and it was agreed to incorporate this revaluation into the company's accounts. It is the company's policy to apply a full year's depreciation in the year of acquisition.
The expected useful life of the extension was to be the same as the remaining useful life of the original building.

You are required to prepare the relevant ledger accounts in respect of the above transactions for the years ended 31 December 2006 to 31 December 2010.

Solution to Question 8.5

Buildings Account

Year		(€)	Year		(€)
2006			**2006**		
1 Jan	Bank	120,000	31 Dec	Balance C/D	120,000
2007			**2007**		
1 Jan	Balance B/D	120,000	31 Dec	Balance C/D	120,000
2008			**2008**		
1 Jan	Balance B/D	120,000	31 Dec	Balance C/D	168,000
	Bank	38,000			
	Wages	10,000			
		168,000			168,000
2009			**2009**		
1 Jan	Balance B/D	168,000	31 Dec	Balance C/D	168,000
2010			**2010**		
1 Jan	Balance B/D	168,000	31 Dec	Balance C/D	230,000
1 Jan	Revaluation Reserve	62,000			
		230,000			230,000

Buildings Accumulated Depreciation Account

Year		(€)	Year		(€)
2006			**2006**		
31 Dec	Balance C/D	2,400	31 Dec	Profit and Loss	2,400
2007			**2007**		
31 Dec	Balance C/D	4,800	1 Jan	Balance B/D	2,400
			31 Dec	Profit and Loss	2,400
		4,800			4,800
2008			**2008**		
31 Dec	Balance C/D	8,300	1 Jan	Balance B/D	4,800
			31 Dec	Profit and Loss	3,500
		8,300			8,300
2009			**2009**		
31 Dec	Balance C/D	11,800	1 Jan	Balance B/D	8,300
			31 Dec	Profit and Loss	3,500
		11,800			11,800
2010			**2010**		
1 Jan	Revaluation Reserve	11,800	1 Jan	Balance B/D	11,800
31 Dec	Balance C/D	5,000	31 Dec	Profit and Loss	5,000
		16,800			16,800

Building Repairs Account

2009		(€)	2009		(€)
1 Jan	Bank	2,000	31 Dec	Profit and Loss	2,000

Revaluation Reserve Account

2010		(€)	2010		(€)
31 Dec	Balance C/D	73,800	1 Jan	Buildings	62,000
			1 Jan	Building Accumulated Depreciation	11,800
		73,800			73,800

9 Control Accounts

It is vital to know **where the figures in control accounts come from**. The figures in the actual control account do not originate in the personal accounts. In fact, they are taken from the **nominal/general ledger accounts**.

Let's go through the **steps affecting debtors**. The approach is then the same for creditors:

key point

In appearance the control is just the same as a personal account, and this causes confusion for some students. You must go back to basic bookkeeping.

1. All credit sales are entered individually in the debtors accounts and the total is entered in the sales accounts.
2. This is the same for returns, payments, discounts, etc.
3. At the end of the period, the accounts are balanced, and a list of all the debtors is drawn up.
4. At this stage only the control account is drawn up. This is done as a check/control on the accuracy of the list of debtors.

5. We go back to the accounts in the nominal ledger and take out the various total figures for the debtors items. These are then entered in the control account, which is balanced.

exam focus

In all the questions in this chapter, differences have arisen – and, as in suspense accounts, you need to reconcile the figures.

6. The balance on the control account is then compared with the total of the list of debtors.

Question 9.1

On 31 December 2010 the creditors ledger control account of F. Short showed the following balances: €19,560 and €360. These did not agree with the list of balances because of the following:

1. An invoice received from K. Fahy for the purchase of goods at €900 less a trade discount of 30 per cent had been omitted from the books. (An item omitted will affect both the list of creditors and the control account, both of which should be increased.)

2. A credit note had been received from a supplier for €245. The only entry made in the books was €254 credited to the creditors account. (This is missing from the purchases returns account, and the figure in the creditors account is both incorrect and on the wrong side.)

3. A discount of €85 was received and omitted from the books. (An omission means both sides must be reduced.)

4. A cash purchase of €300 had been credited to a supplier's account. (Cash purchases do not belong here at all.)

5. A creditor had charged Short €75 interest on an overdue account. The only entry made in the books had been €57 credited in the creditors account. Following a complaint made by Short, this charge was reduced to €40 but had not been entered in the books. (In interest account, enter €40, and reduce creditors account to €40.)

6. A credit note received from a supplier for €150 had been debited twice in the purchases returns account but omitted from the creditors account. (With purchases returns on the wrong side twice, a correction is then needed, and a reduction in creditors account must be entered.)

You are required to show:

(a) The adjusted creditors control account.

(b) The adjusted list of creditors.

(c) A journal entry to correct error 5.

Solution to Question 9.1

F. Short
(a) Adjusted Creditors Control Account

	(€)		(€)
Balance	360	Balance	19,560
Credit Note (2)	245	K. Fahy (1)	630
Discount Received (3)	85	Interest (5)	40
Balance C/D	20,050	Credit Note (6)	150
		Balance	360
	20,740		20,740
Balance C/D	360	Balance B/D	20,050

(b) Adjusted List of Creditors

	Plus (€)	Minus (€)	(€)
Original Balance			20,111
K. Fahy (1)	630		
Credit Note (2)		(499)	
Discount Received (3)		(85)	
Cash Purchases (4)		(300)	
Interest (5)		(17)	
Credit Note (6)		(150)	
	+630	(1,051)	(421)
Corrected Balance			19,690

(c) Journal Entry

	Dr (€)	Cr (€)
Creditors	17	
Interest	40	
Suspense		57

Interest omitted from interest account and inverted figure in creditors account.

Question 9.2

On 31 December 2010 the creditors ledger control account of P. Flynn showed the following balances: €26,940 and €140. These figures did not agree with the schedule (list) of creditors drawn up. An examination of the books revealed the following.

1. A credit note received for €340 had been entered in the books as €430.
2. Goods purchased on credit for €1,800 had been omitted from the books.
3. A discount received of €70 had been entered correctly. This had been subsequently disallowed, and the only entry made in the books had been €70 debited to the creditors account.
4. A cash purchase of €300 had been credited to the creditors account.
5. Bills payable accepted of €900 had been entered twice in the creditors account.
6. Flynn won a holiday voucher valued at €3,000. She gave half of this to a creditor as part-payment of her account. No entry had been made in the books.

You are required to show:

(a) The adjusted creditors control account.

(b) The adjusted list of creditors.

Solution to Question 9.2

P. Flynn
(a) Adjusted Creditors Control Account

	(€)		(€)
Balance	140	Balance	26,940
Holiday Voucher (6)	1,500	Credit Note (1)	90
Balance C/D	27,400	Purchases (2)	1,800
		Discount Received (3)	70
		Balance C/D	140
	29,040		29,040
Balance B/D	140	Balance B/D	27,400

(b) Adjusted List of Creditors

	Plus (€)	Minus (€)	(€)
Original Balance			26,130
Credit Note (1)	90		
Purchases (2)	1,800		
Discount Received (3)	140		
Cash Purchases (4)		300	
Bills Payable (5)	900		
Holiday Voucher (6)		1,500	
	2,930	(1,800)	+1,130
Correct Balance			27,260

Question 9.3

On 31 December 2011 the debtors ledger control account of B. Cunningham showed balances of €25,560 and €80. These figures did not agree with the list of debtors drawn up on the same date. An examination of the books revealed the following.

1. An invoice sent to a customer for €750 had been entered in the day books as €570.
2. Interest of €85 had been charged to a customer but had been entered as €95 in the customer's account. Following a complaint by the customer, this had been reduced to €40 but had not been entered in the books.

3. Cash sales of €6,000 had been debited to a customer's account.
4. A discount of €30 was disallowed but had been treated as allowed in the customers account.
5. Sales returns of €400 had been omitted from the books.
6. A credit note for €150 was sent to a customer and entered in the books. The clerk forgot to deduct 10 per cent for a restocking charge and then sent and entered a second credit note for €135.

You are required to show:

(a) The adjusted debtors ledger control account.
(b) The adjusted schedule of debtors.

Solution to Question 9.3

B. Cunningham
(a) Adjusted Debtors Control Account

	(€)		(€)
Balance	25,560	Balance	80
Credit Note (6)	150		
Invoice (1)	180	Interest (2)	45
		Sales Returns (5)	400
		Balance C/D	25,365
	25,890		25,890
Balance B/D	25,365		

(b) Adjusted List of Debtors

	Plus (€)	Minus (€)	(€)
Original Balance			31,430
Invoice (1)	180		
Interest (2)		(55)	
Cash Sales (3)		(6,000)	
Discount Disallowed (4)	60		
Sales Returns (5)		(400)	
Credit Note (6)	150		
	(390)	(6,455)	(6,065)
Correct Balance			25,365 (starting point)

Question 9.4

The debtors ledger control account of R. Gilmartin showed the following balances: €18,840 debit and €390 credit on 31 December 2010. These figures did not agree with the schedule (list) of debtors balances extracted on the same date. An examination of the books revealed the following.

1. Interest amounting to €64, charged to a customer's overdue account, had been entered as €46 in the interest account. Following a complaint by the customer, this charge was reduced to €36, but this reduction had not been entered in the books.

2. A discount to a customer of €15 was disallowed and had been treated as a discount allowed in the discount account.

3. Gilmartin had sent an invoice to a customer for €870. This had been entered in the appropriate day book as €780. However, when posting from this book to the ledger, no entry had been made in the personal account.

4. Bills payable of €750 had been entered on the debit side of a debtor's account.

5. A credit note was sent to a customer for €105. The only entry made in the books was €15 debited to the debtors account.

6. A customer's account had been credited with cash sales of €425.

7. A credit note for €160 was sent to a customer and entered in the books. However, the accounts clerk forgot to deduct a restocking charge of 10 per cent. When the error was realised, the clerk immediately sent another credit note for €144 and debited it to the debtors account.

You are required to show:

(a) The adjusted debtors ledger control account.

(b) The adjusted schedule of debtors showing the original balance.

Solution to Question 9.4

(a) Adjusted Debtors Ledger Control Account

	(€)		(€)
Balance	18,840	Balance	390
Discount Disallowed (2)	30	Interest (1)	10
Invoice Error (3)	90	Credit Note Omitted (5)	105
Credit Note Error (7)	16	Balance	18,861
Balance	390		
	€19,366		€19,366
Balance B/D	18,861	Balance B/D	390

(b) Adjusted Schedule of Debtors

	(€)	(€)
Balance as per List		18,202
Add Invoice Omitted (3)	870	
Cash Sales (6)	425	1,295
		19,497
Deduct Interest (1)	28	
Bills Payable (4)	750	
Credit Note Error (6)	120	
Restocking Error (7)	128	1,026
Balance as per Adjusted Control Account		18,471

10 Cash Flow Statements

There is more to answering questions about cash flow statements than merely understanding their layout. In Section 2, i.e. the 100-mark question, you may also be required to prepare an abridged profit and loss account – in which case, write out the layout first. You then start at the bottom figure, which is the retained profit at year-end, and work backwards to find the operating profit figure. Remember to add back the figures that you would normally subtract.

key point

It is essential that you know the layout for cash flow statements. The layout used is provided in the solutions. Write it out blank first when answering these questions.

In reconciling the operating profit to the net cash flow, the following always apply:

1. Always add back depreciation.

2. Profit on disposal is a minus and loss is a plus.

3. Increase in stock and debtors is a minus and decrease is a plus.

4. Increase in creditors is a plus and decrease is a minus.

In the cash flow statement itself, all the figures are payments or receipts. The interest figure is calculated as a percentage of the loan figure. The taxation and dividends are best calculated using T accounts. The rest of the figures are the difference between the two balance sheets.

In reconciling the net cash and net debt, start with the final figure in the cash flow statement, i.e. the increase/decrease in cash, and adjust this with the increase/decrease in debentures. The final figure is the net debt at the end of the year, which is checked by comparing the loans and cash at end of year.

These are dealt with in the sample questions here.

exam focus

There is usually a short theory question to finish, typically something like:

1. Why prepare cash flow statements?
2. What are non-cash items?
3. Why does an increase in profit not mean an increase in cash?

Question 10.1

The following are the balance sheets of McGarry Plc as at 31/12/2009 and 31/12/2010.

	31/12/2009		31/12/2010	
	€	€	€	€
Fixed Assets				
Cost	600,000		520,000	
Less Accumulated Depreciation	140,000		120,000	
	460,000		400,000	
Quoted Investments	150,000		80,000	
		610,000		480,000
Current Assets				
Stock	390,000		310,000	
Debtors	190,000		210,000	
	580,000		520,000	
Less Creditors Amounts Falling Due within One Year				
Trade Creditors	200,000		170,000	
Bank	20,000		35,000	
Taxation	40,000		25,000	
Dividends	70,000		60,000	
	330,000		290,000	
Net Current Assets		250,000		230,000
		860,000		710,000
Financed by				
Creditors: Amounts Falling Due after More Than One Year				
8% Debentures	240,000		200,000	
Capital and Reserves				
Ordinary Shares	350,000		300,000	
Share Premium	10,000		—	
Profit and Loss Account	260,000		210,000	
		860,000		710,000

The following information is also available:

1. 50,000 shares were issued at €120 per share.
2. €40,000 debentures were issued on 30/6/2009.
3. Fixed assets which cost €60,000 and on which total depreciation of €40,000 had been provided were sold for €30,000.
4. Dividends due and taxation due on 31/12/2009 were paid. Interim dividends for 2010 of €50,000 were also paid.

You are required to:

(a) Prepare an abridged profit and loss account for the year ending 31/12/2010.

(b) Reconcile the operating profit to net cash inflow from operating activities.

Solution to Question 10.1

(a) Abridged Profit and Loss Account for the Year Ending 31 December 2010

	€000	€000	
Operating Profit		227.6	last figure
Less Interest Note 1		(17.6)	
		210	
Less Taxation		(40)	
		170	
Less Dividends: Interim	(50)		
Proposed	(70)	(120)	
Retained Profit		50	
Balance 1/1/2010		210	2nd figure
Balance 31/12/2010		260	1st figure

Note 1

Interest $€200,000 \times 8\% \times \dfrac{6}{12} = €8,000$

$€240,000 \times 8\% \times \dfrac{6}{12} = €9,600$

Total $€17,600$

(b) Reconciliation of Operating Profit to Net Cash Inflow from Operating Activities

Operating Profit	227.6
Plus Depreciation	60
Less Profit on Disposal	(10)
Less Increase in Stock	(80)
Plus Decrease in Debtors	20
Plus Increase in Creditors	30
Net Cash Inflow from Operating Activities	247.6

Note: Net debt at 1/1/2010 = Debentures 200 + Bank 35

Net debt at 31/12/2010 = Debentures 240 + Bank 20

Notes

Fixed Asset Account

1/1	Balance	520		Disposal	60
	Bank cfs	140	31/12	Balance	600
		660			660

Accumulated Depreciation Account

	Disposal	40	1/1	Balance	120
31/12	Balance	140		Profit and Loss cfs	60
		180			180

Disposal Account

Fixed Assets	60		Acc. Depn.	40
Profit and Loss cfs	10		Bank cfs	30
	70			70

Theory

Why prepare cash flow statements?

1. Because they may be compulsory.

2. Because profits do not equal cash.

3. To find out what happened to cash during the year.

4. To help predict future cash flows.

What are non-cash items?

These are things that do not affect cash. These include depreciation, provisions for bad debts, either an increase or decrease and profits or losses on disposals.

Why does profit not always equal cash?

1. Goods may be sold on credit at a profit.

2. Non-cash items affect profit but not cash.

3. Acquisitions and disposals may affect cash but not profit.

Question 10.2

The following are the balance sheets of Experience Plc as at 31/12/2010 and 31/12/2009.

	31/12/2010		31/12/2009	
	€	€	€	€
Fixed Assets				
Cost	500,000		480,000	
Less Accumulated Depreciation	(120,000)	380,000	(110,000)	370,000
Current Assets				
Stock	369,000		310,000	
Debtors	181,000		118,000	
	550,000		428,000	
Less Creditors: Amounts Falling Due within One Year				
Trade Creditors	170,000		190,000	
Bank	10,000		34,000	
Taxation	38,000		29,000	
Dividends	52,000		65,000	
	270,000		318,000	
Net Current Assets		280,000		110,000
		660,000		480,000
Financed by				
Creditors: Amounts Falling Due after More than One Year				
10% Debentures		150,000		100,000
Capital and Reserves				
€1 Ordinary Shares		260,000		200,000
Share Premium		12,000		—
Profit and Loss Account		238,000		180,000
		660,000		480,000

The following information is also available:
1. 60,000 shares were issued at €1.20 per share.
2. Fixed assets, which cost €50,000 and on which total depreciation of €25,000 had been provided, were sold for €30,000.
3. €50,000 debentures were issued on 1/1/2010.
4. Dividends due and taxation due on 31/12/2009 were paid.

You are required to:

(a) Prepare an abridged profit and loss account to ascertain the operating profit for the year ending 31/12/2010. `25`

(b) Reconcile the operating profit to net cash inflow from operating activities. `25`

(c) Prepare the cash flow statement for Experience Plc for the year ended 31/12/2010. `35`

(d) Explain why cash flow statements are prepared. `15`

`100 marks`

Solution to Question 10.2 `25`

(a) Abridged Profit and Loss Account for the Year Ended 31/12/2010

	€
Operating Profit	163,000 ❺
Interest Paid	(15,000) ❹
Profit before Taxation	148,000
Taxation	(38,000) ❹
Profit after Taxation	110,000
Proposed Dividends	(52,000)
Retained Profits for the Year	58,000 ❸
Profit and Loss Balance 1/1/2010	180,000
Profit and Loss Balance 31/12/2010	238,000

(b) Reconciliation of Operating Profit to Net Cash Flow from Operating Activities `25`

	Workings	€
Operating Profit		163,000 ❸
Depreciation Charges for Year	W1	35,000 ❺
Profit on Sale of Fixed Assets	W2	(5,000) ❺
Increase in Stocks		(59,000) ❸
Increase in Debtors		(63,000) ❸
Decrease in Creditors		(20,000) ❸
Net Cash Inflow from Operating Activities		51,000 ❸

(c) Cash Flow Statement of Experience Plc for the Year Ended 31/12/2010   35

	€	€
Operating Activities		
Net Cash Inflow from Operating Activities		51,000 ❶
Returns on Investment and Servicing of Finance ❷		
Interest Paid	(15,000) ❷	
Dividends Paid	(65,000) ❸	(80,000)
Taxation ❷		
Corporation Tax Paid		(29,000) ❸
Investing Activities ❷		
Payments to Acquire Tangible Fixed Assets W3	(70,000) ❹	
Receipts from Sale of Fixed Assets	30,000 ❷	(40,000)
Net Cash Outflow before Financing ❶		(98,000)
Financing ❷		
Receipts from Issue of Debentures	50,000 ❸	
Receipts from Issue of Shares	60,000 ❸	
Receipts from Share Premium	12,000 ❸	122,000
Increase in Cash ❶		24,000 ❶

(d)   3 × 5 marks (15)

- To show the cash inflows and outflows during the past year.
- To help predict future cash flows.
- To help financial planning.
- To provide information to assess liquidity.
- To show that profits do not equal cash.
- To comply with legal requirements.

Workings

1. **Depreciation**

Depreciation Provision at 31/12/2010	120,000
Less Depreciation Provision at 1/1/2010	110,000
Increase in Provision	10,000
Depreciation Transferred to Disposal	25,000
Depreciation for Year	35,000

2. **Profit on Disposal of Fixed Assets**

Net Book Value of Fixed Assets Sold (50,000 – 25,000)	25,000
Proceeds on Disposal	30,000
Profit on Disposal of Fixed Assets	5,000

3. **Assets Purchased**

Fixed Assets at the Beginning of the Year	480,000
Less Fixed Assets Sold during Year	50,000
	430,000
Add Fixed Assets Purchased during the Year	70,000
Fixed Assets at the End of the Year	50,000

Question 10.3

The following are the balance sheets of Creation Plc as at 31/12/2009 and 31/12/2010 together with an abridged profit and loss account for the year ended 31/12/2010.

Abridged Profit and Loss Account for the Year Ended 31/12/2010

		€
Operating Profit		150,600
Interest for Year		(10,600)
Profit before Taxation		140,000
Taxation for Year		(47,000)
Profit after Taxation		93,000
Dividends – Interim	23,000	
– Proposed	48,000	(71,000)
Retained Profits for the Year		22,000
Retained Profits on 1/12/2010		189,000
Retained Profits on 31/12/2010		211,000

Balance Sheets as at

	31/12/2010		31/12/2009	
	€	€	€	€
Fixed Assets				
Land and Buildings at Cost	800,000		725,000	
Less Accumulated Depreciation	(75,000)	725,000	(60,000)	665,000
Machinery at Cost	380,000		450,000	
Less Accumulated Depreciation	(190,000)	190,000	(170,000)	280,000
		915,000		945,000

Financial Assets				
Quoted Investments		120,000		90,000
Current Assets				
Stock		225,000		208,000
Debtors		212,000		184,000
Bank		—		12,000
Cash		3,000		1,000
		440,000		405,000
Less Creditors: Amounts Falling Due within One Year				
Trade Creditors	253,000		230,000	
Interest Due	1,400		—	
Taxation	51,000		44,000	
Dividends	48,000		37,000	
Bank	8,600		—	
	(362,000)		(311,000)	
Net Current Assets		78,000		94,000
		1,113,000		1,129,000
Financed by				
Creditors: Amounts Falling Due after More than One Year				
8% Debentures		50,000		160,000
Capital and Reserves				
€1 Ordinary Shares	840,000		780,000	
Share Premium	12,000		—	
Profit and Loss Account	211,000	1,063,000	189,000	969,000
		1,113,000		1,129,000

The following information is also available:

1. There were no disposals of buildings during the year, but new buildings were acquired.
2. There were no purchases of machinery during the year. Machinery was disposed of for €24,000.
3. Depreciation charged for the year on machinery in arriving at the operating profit was €55,000.

You are required to:

(a) Reconcile the operating profit to net cash inflow from operating activities. **20**

(b) Prepare the cash flow statement of Creation Plc for the year ended 31/12/2010. **30**

(c) Explain why profit does not always mean a corresponding increase in cash and list two non-cash items. **10**

60 marks

Solution to Question 10.3 [20]

(a) Reconciliation of Operating Profit to Net Cash Flow from Operating Activities

	Workings	€
Operating Profit		150,600 ❷
Depreciation Charges for Year	W1	70,000 ❹
Loss on Sale of Machinery	W2	11,000 ❻
Increase in Stocks		(17,000) ❷
Increase in Stocks		(28,000) ❷
Increase in Creditors		23,000 ❷
Net Cash Inflow from Operating Activities		209,600 ❷

(b) Cash Flow Statement of Creation Plc for the Year Ended 31/12/2010 [30]

	Workings	€
Operating Activities		
Net Cash Inflow from Operating Activities		209,600 ❶
Returns on Investment and Servicing of Finance ❶		
Interest Paid		(9,200) ❸
Taxation ❷		
Corporation Tax Paid		(40,000) ❸
Capital Expenditure and Financial Investment ❶		
Investments	(30,000) ❷	
Payments to Acquire Tangible Fixed Assets	(75,000) ❷	
Receipts from Sale of Fixed Assets	24,000 ❷	(81,000)
Equity Dividends Paid ❶		
Dividends Paid during Year	W3	(60,000) ❹
Net Cash **Inflow** before Liquid Resources and Financing		19,400
Financing		
Repayment of Debentures	(110,000) ❷	
Receipts from Issue of Shares	60,000 ❶	
Receipts from Share Premium	12,000 ❶	(38,000)
Decrease in Cash ❷		18,600
Reconciliation of Net Cash Flow to Movement in Net Debt		
Decrease in Cash during Period		(18,600) ❶
Cash Used to Purchase Debentures		110,000 ❶
Change in Net Debt		91,400
Net Debt at 1/1/2010		(147,000)
Net Debt at 31/12/2010		555,600 ❶

(c)   `10`

- Credit sales/purchases affect profit but do not affect cash.
- Non-cash losses and gains affect profit but not cash.
- Purchase and sale of fixed assets by cash affect cash but not profit.
- Introduction or withdrawal of capital in cash affects cash but not profit.
- Non-cash items – depreciation, provisions against losses, losses/profits from sale of assets.

11 Published Accounts

The layout of these questions must be exactly followed. This should be written out in **blank form** first. NB: The layout is as shown in the sample questions.

1. Profit and loss account

(a) The title is 'profit and loss account'.

(b) The word 'turnover', not 'sales', is to be used.

(c) Cost of sales is calculated separately and is shown as one figure.

(d) Distribution and administrative expenses are shown each as one figure.

(e) The dividends must be shown as paid and proposed.

(f) The other figures are usually quite straightforward.

2. Balance sheet

(a) Fixed assets must be shown under intangible, tangible and financial.

(b) Current assets must be listed in full.

(c) Liabilities are shown under creditors due within one year and after more than one year.

(d) The capital section is shown as usual.

3. Notes to the accounts

The usual notes asked for are:

(a) Accounting policy.

(b) Operating profit.

(c) Tangible fixed assets.

(d) Dividends.

exam focus

There are a lot of marks for this section. There is usually a fifth note required, which is often an explanation in simple English of what is asked. Learn these from the solutions. In the note on dividends, you are required to show the amount in cents per share and in total.

Question 11.1

Gayle Plc has an authorised capital of €800,000 divided into 600,000 ordinary shares at €1 each and 200,000 nine per cent preference shares at €1 each. The following trial balance was extracted from its books at 31/12/2010.

	€	€
Vehicles at Cost	220,000	
Vehicles – Accumulated Dep on 1/1/2010		33,000
Investment Income		10,000
Buildings at Cost	700,000	
Buildings – Accumulated Dep on 1/1/2010		42,000
Debtors and Creditors	289,000	163,000
9% Investments	240,000	
Stock at 1/1/2010	73,000	
Patent at 1/1/2010	40,000	
Administration Expenses	172,000	
Purchases and Sales	1,150,000	1,880,000
Rental Income		60,000
8% Debentures 2009/2010		200,000
Distribution Costs	248,000	
Profit on Sale of Land		65,000
Bank	48,000	
VAT		71,000
Interim Dividends	24,000	
Profit and Loss at 1/1/2010		52,000
Issued Capital		
Ordinary Shares		400,000
Preference Shares		200,000
Provision for Bad Debts		27,000
Debenture Interest Paid	12,000	
Discount		13,000
	3,216,000	3,216,000

The following information is relevant:

1. Stock on 31/12/2010 is €96,000.
2. The patent was acquired on 1/1/2010 for €80,000. It is being amortised over eight years in equal instalments. The amortisation is to be included in cost of sales.
3. On 1/7/2010, the ordinary shareholders received an interim dividend of €15,000 and the preference shareholders received €9,000. The directors propose the payment of the preference dividend due and a final dividend on ordinary shares to bring that total dividend up to 7c per share.

4. Provide for debenture interest due, investment interest due, auditors' fees €9,500, directors' fees €50,000 and corporation tax €87,000.

5. Depreciation is to be provided for on buildings at a rate of two per cent straight line and is to be allocated 20 per cent on distribution costs and 80 per cent on administration expenses. There was no purchase or sale of buildings during the year. Vehicles are to be depreciated at the rate of 20 per cent of cost.

6. During the year, land adjacent to the company's premises, which had cost €80,000, was sold for €145,000. At the end of the year the company revalued its buildings at €900,000. The company wishes to incorporate this value in this year's accounts.

7. Included in administration expenses is the receipt of €12,000 for patent royalties.

You are required to:

(a) Prepare the published profit and loss account for the year 31/12/2010 and a balance sheet as at that date, in accordance with the Companies Acts and appropriate accounting standards, showing the following notes:

  (i) Accounting policy note for tangible fixed assets and stock.
  (ii) Operating profit.
  (iii) Interest payable.
  (iv) Dividends.
  (v) Tangible fixed assets.   84

(b) State three items of information that must be included in a directors' report.   9

(c) Explain the term 'exceptional item' and give an example.   7

100 marks

Solution to Question 11.1   36

(a) Profit and Loss Account of Gayle Plc for Year Ended 31/12/2010

	€
Turnover	1,880,000 ❷
Cost of Sales	(1,137,000) ❹
Gross Profit	743,000
Distribution Costs	(294,800) ❸
	448,200
Administrative Expenses	(254,700) ❺
	193,500
Other Operating Income	85,000 ❸
Operating Profit ❶	278,500
Investment Income	21,600 ❷
Profit on Sale of Land	65,000 ❷
	365,100

	€
Interest Payable	(16,000) ❸
Profit on Ordinary Activities before Tax	349,100
Taxation	(87,000) ❷
	262,100
Dividend Paid (24,000) ❸	
Dividend Proposed (22,000) ❸	(46,000)
	216,100
Profit Brought Forward at 1/1/2011	52,000 ❷
Profit Carried Forward at 31/12/2011	268,100 ❶

Workings

Cost of Sales	73,000 + 1,150,000 + 10,000 − 96,000	= 1,137,000
Distribution Costs	248,000 + 2,800 + 44,000	= 294,800
Administrative Expenses	172,000 + 9,500 + 50,000 + 11,200 + 12,000	= 254,700
Other Operating Income	60,000 + 13,000 + 12,000	= 85,000
Debtors	289,000 − 27,000 + 11,600	= 273,600

Balance Sheet of Gayle Plc as at 31/12/2010   27

			€
Fixed Assets			
Intangible Assets			30,000 ❷
Tangible Assets			1,043,000 ❷
Financial Assets			240,000 ❶
			1,313,000
Current Assets			
Stock	96,000 ❶		
Debtors	273,600 ❸		
Bank	48,000 ❶	417,600	
Creditors: Amounts Falling Due within One Year: ❶			
Trade Creditors	163,000 ❶		
Dividends Due	22,000 ❷		
Taxation	158,000 ❷		
Other Creditors	63,500 ❹		
		(406,500)	
Net Current Assets			11,100
Total Assets less Current Liabilities			1,324,100
Creditors: Amounts Falling Due after More than One Year			
8% Debentures			200,000 ❶

Capital and Reserves		
Issued Shares	600,000 ❷	
Revaluation Reserve	256,000 ❸	
Profit Carried Forward	268,100 ❶	
		1,124,000
		1,324,100

Notes to the Accounts

Accounting Policy Notes ⬛21

(i) Tangible Fixed Assets ❻

Buildings were revalued at the end of 2010 and have been included in the accounts at their revalued amount. Vehicles are shown at cost. Depreciation is calculated in order to write off the value of the tangible assets over their estimated useful economic life, as follows:

- Buildings: two per cent per annum – straight-line basis.
- Delivery vans: 20 per cent of cost.
- Stocks: Stocks are valued on a first in, first out basis at the lower of cost and net realisable value.

(ii) Operating Profit ❸

Operating profit is arrived at after charging:

Depreciation on Tangible Assets	58,000
Patent Amortised	10,000

(iii) Interest Payable ❷

Interest payable on debentures (repayable by 2014/2015) 16,000

(iv) Dividends ❹

Ordinary Dividends

Interim/Paid 3.75c per share	15,000	
Final Proposed 3.25c per share	13,000	28,000

Preference Dividends

Interim/Paid 4.5c per share	9,000	
Final Proposed 4.5c per share	9,000	18,000

(v) Tangible Fixed Assets ❻

	Land and Buildings	Vehicles	Total
1/1/2010	780,000	220,000	1,000,000
Disposal	(80,000)		(80,000)
Revaluation Surplus 31/12/2010	200,000		200,000
Value at 31/12/2010	900,000	220,000	1,120,000
Depreciation 1/1/2010	42,000	33,000	75,000
Depreciation Charge for Year	14,000	44,000	58,000
	56,000	77,000	133,000
Transfer on Revaluation	(56,000)		(56,000)
Depreciation 31/12/2010	Nil	7 7,000	77,000
Net Book Value 1/1/2010	738,000	187,000	925,000
Net Book Value 31/12/2010	900,000	143,000	1,043,000

(b)

Directors' Report 3 × 3 marks   9

A directors' report must contain the following:

- The dividends recommended for payment.
- The amount to be transferred to reserves.
- A report of any changes in the nature of the company's business during the year.
- A fair review of the development of the business of the company during the year and of the position at the end of the year.
- The principal activities of the company and any changes therein.
- Details of any important events affecting the company since the end of the year.
- Any likely future developments in the business.
- An indication of activities in the field of research and development.
- Significant changes in fixed assets.
- Details of own shares purchased.
- A list of the company's subsidiaries and affiliates.
- Evaluation of company's compliance with its safety statement.
- Details of directors' shareholdings and dealings during the year.

(c)   9

Exceptional Item

This is a material item of significant size. It is a profit or loss that must be shown separately in the profit and loss account because of size. ❹

Example: Profit or loss on sale of fixed asset or large bad debt. ❸

Question 11.2

The following is the trial balance of Thompson Plc as at 31/12/2010.

	Dr €	Cr €
Fixed Asset Investments	300,000	
Patent at 1/1/2007	168,000	
Building – Cost at 1/1/2010	700,000	
Building – Accumulated Depreciation at 1/1/2010		48,000
Stock at 1/1/2010	650,000	
Debtors and Creditors	139,000	241,000
8% Debentures 2014/2015		400,000
Purchases and Sales	6,150,000	7,988,000
Distribution Costs	610,000	
Administration Expenses	742,000	
Rental Income		52,000
Provision for Bad Debts		23,000
Debenture Interest Paid	12,000	
Interim Dividends	24,000	
Profit on the Sale of Land		80,000
Bank	179,000	
VAT		82,000
Authorised and Issued Share Capital:		
Ordinary Shares @ €1 Each		400,000
7% Preference Shares @ €1 Each		300,000
Profit and Loss at 1/1/2010		60,000
	9,674,000	9,674,000

The following additional information is provided:

1. Stock at 31/12/2010 is €690,000.

2. Depreciation is to be provided for as follows:

   Building: two per cent straight-line (there were no purchases or sales of buildings during the year).

   During the year, land adjacent to the company's building which had cost €55,000 was sold for €135,000. At the end of the year the company revalued its building at €750,000.

   The company wishes to incorporate this value in this year's accounts.

3. Provision is to be made for:

   Directors' remuneration €80,000.

   Auditors' remuneration €9,000.

   Corporation tax €170,000.

   Debenture interest due at 31/12/2010.

4. The patent was acquired on 1/1/2007 for €240,000. It is being amortised over 10 years in equal instalments. The amortisation should be included in cost of sales.

5. On 1 July 2010 interim dividends of €10,500 and €13,500 were paid to the ordinary and preference shareholders, respectively. The directors propose the payment of the preference dividend due and a final dividend on ordinary shares of 6c per share.

6. The fixed asset investments are in listed companies. The market value of these investments at 31/12/2010 was €480,000. There were no purchases or sales of investments during the year.

7. The debentures are secured by a fixed charge over the company's tangible fixed assets.

8. On 12/12/2010 the company received a letter from a former employee who was dismissed on 1/10/2010. The employee is claiming compensation for unlawful dismissal. The company's legal advisers believe that the company is unlikely to be liable under the terms of the employment contract and they estimate the maximum amount of the liability will be legal costs of €25,000.

You are required to:

(a) Prepare the published profit and loss account for the year ended 31/12/2010 and a balance sheet as at that date in accordance with the Companies Acts and latest accounting standards, showing the following notes:

   (i) Accounting policy note for tangible fixed assets and stock.

   (ii) Operating profit.

   (iii) Contingent liabilities.

   (iv) Dividends.

   (v) Tangible fixed assets.   **85**

(b) State the difference between an auditor's qualified and unqualified report.   **15**

100 marks

Solution to Question 11.2 `45`

(a) Profit and Loss Account of Thompson Plc for the Year Ended 31/12/2010

	Notes	€
Turnover ❶		7,988,000 ❷
Cost of Sales	1	6,134,000 ❻
Gross Profit		1,854,000
Distribution Costs		(610,000) ❶
Administrative Expenses		(845,000) ❽
		399,000
Other Operating Income		
Rental Income		52,000 ❷
Operating Profit ❶	2	451,000
Profit on Sale of Land		80,000 ❷
		531,000
Interest Payable	3	(32,000) ❹
Profit on Ordinary Activities before Taxation ❶		499,000
Taxation on Profit on Ordinary Activities		(170,000) ❷
Profit on Ordinary Activities after Taxation		329,000
Dividends Paid	4	(24,000) ❹
Dividends Proposed	4	(31,500) ❹
Profit Retained for Year		273,500
Profit Brought Forward at 1/1/2010		60,000
Profit Carried Forward at 31/12/2010		333,500 ❹

Balance Sheet as at 31/12/2010 `22`

Fixed Assets	Notes			
Intangible Assets			144,000 ❸	
Tangible Assets	5		750,000 ❷	
Financial			300,000 ❶	1,194,000
Current Assets				
Stock		690,000 ❶		
Debtors		116,000 ❶		
Cash at Bank and On Hand		179,000 ❶	985,000	
Creditors: Amounts Falling Due within One Year				
Trade Creditors		241,000 ❶		
Other Creditors		109,000 ❶		
Taxation and Social Welfare		252,000 ❷		
Proposed Dividends		31,500 ❶	633,500	

Net Current Assets		351,500
Total Assets less Current Liabilities		1,545,500 ❷
Creditors: Amounts Falling Due after More than One Year		
8% Debentures 2014/2015		400,000 ❷
Capital and Reserves		
Called-Up Share Capital	700,000 ❷	
Revaluation Reserve	112,000 ❸	
Profit and Loss Account	333,500 ❶	1,145,500
		1,545,500

Notes to the Accounts

18

Accounting policy notes ❺

(i) **Tangible Fixed Assets**

Buildings were revalued at the end of 2010 and have been included in the accounts at their revalued amount. Depreciation is calculated in order to write off the value or cost of tangible fixed assets over their estimated useful economic life, as follows:

- Buildings: two per cent per annum – straight-line basis.
- Stocks: Stocks are valued on a first in, first out basis at the lower of cost and net realisable value.

(ii) **Operating profit** ❸

The operating profit is arrived at after charging:

Depreciation on Tangible Fixed Assets	14,000
Patent Amortised	24,000
Directors' Remuneration	80,000
Auditors' Remuneration	9,000

(iii) **Contingent Liability** ❷

The company is being sued by a former employee for unlawful dismissal. The company's legal advisers have advised that the company will probably *not* be liable under the terms of the employment contract. They have estimated the maximum amount of liability at €25,000.

(iv) **Dividends** ❹

Ordinary Dividends		
Interim Paid 2.625c per Share	10,500	
Final Proposed 60c per Share	24,000	34,500
Preference Dividends		
Interim Paid 45c per Share	13,500	
Final Proposed 2.5c per Share	7,500	21,000
		55,500

(v) Tangible Fixed Assets ❹	Land and Buildings	Total
Cost/Valuation at 1/1/2010	755,000	755,000
Disposal	55,000	55,000
Revaluation Surplus at 31/12/2010	50,000	50,000
	750,000	750,000
Depreciation at 1/1/2010	48,000	48,000
Charge for Year	14,000	14,000
Transfer on Revaluation	(62,000)	(62,000)
Net Book Values at 31/12/2009	707,000	707,000
Net Book Values at 31/12/2010	750,000	750,000

Workings

Cost of Sales	6,150,000 + 650,000 − 690,000 + 24,000 = 6,134,000
Administrative Expenses	742,000 + 14,000 + 80,000 + 9,000 = 845,000
Revaluation Reserve	48,000 + 50,000 + 14,000 = 112,000

(b) 15

Unqualified Auditor's Report

An unqualified auditor's report is often referred to as a clean report. ❺ This is when the auditor's report states that in his/her opinion the following apply:

- The financial statements *give a true and fair view* ❸ of the state of affairs of the company at the end of the year and of its profit and loss account for the year.
- The financial statements are prepared in accordance with the Companies Acts. ❺
- All the information necessary for the audit was available.
- The information given by the directors is consistent with the financial statements.
- The net assets are more than 50 per cent of the called-up capital.

Qualified Auditor's Report

A qualified auditor's report is when an auditor in his/her opinion is *not satisfied* or is unable to conclude that all or any of the following apply: ❷

- The financial statements give a *true and fair view* of the state of affairs of the company at the end of the year and of its profit and loss account for the year.
- The financial statements are prepared in accordance with the Companies Acts.
- All the information necessary for the audit was available.
- The information given by the directors is consistent with the financial statements.
- The net assets are more than 50 per cent of the called-up capital.

The report will state the elements of the accounts or of the directors' report that are unsatisfactory.

Question 11.3

Oatfield Plc has an authorised capital of €900,000 divided into 700,000 ordinary shares at €1 each and 200,000 eight per cent preference shares at €1 each. The following trial balance was extracted from its books on 31/12/2010.

	€	€
Patent	56,000	
9% Investments 1/1/2010	120,000	
Land and Buildings (revalued on 1/7/2010)	880,000	
Revaluation Reserve		260,000
Delivery Vans at Cost	145,000	
Delivery Vans – Accumulated Depreciation on 1/1/2010		68,000
Debtors and Creditors	187,000	98,000
Purchases and Sales	696,000	1,105,000
Stocks 1/1/2010	75,000	
Directors' Fees	84,000	
Salaries and General Expenses	177,000	
Discount		6,160
Advertising	21,000	
Investment Income		8,100
Profit on Sale of Land		85,000
Rent	32,000	
Interim Dividends for First 6 Months	27,000	
Profit and Loss Balance 1/1/2010		73,700
8% Debentures (2016/2017) Including €120,000 8% Debentures Issued on 1/8/2010		270,000
Bank		17,740
VAT		8,300
Issued Capital		
350,000 Ordinary Shares at €1 Each		350,000
150,000 8% Preference Shares		150,000
	2,500,000	2,500,000

The following information is also relevant:

1. Stock on 31/12/2010 was valued on a first in, first out basis at €77,000.
2. The patent was acquired on 1/1/2007 for €80,000. It is being amortised over 10 years in equal instalments. The amortisation should be included in cost of sales.
3. On 1/7/2010 the ordinary shareholders received an interim dividend of €21,000 and the preference shareholders received €6,000. The directors propose the payment of the preference dividend due and a final dividend on ordinary shares, bringing the total ordinary dividend up to 16c per share for the year.

4. On 1/7/2010 land which had cost €90,000 was sold for €175,000. On this date the remaining land and buildings were revalued at €880,000. Included in this revaluation is land now valued at €180,000 but which originally cost €70,000. The revalued buildings had cost €550,000.

5. Depreciation is to be provided as follows: Delivery vans at the rate of 20 per cent of cost. Buildings at the rate of two per cent of cost per annum until date of revaluation and thereafter at two per cent per annum of revalued figure.

6. Provide for debenture interest due, investment income due, auditors' fees €7,700 and taxation €33,000.

You are required to:

(a) Prepare the published profit and loss account for the year ended 31/12/2010 in accordance with the Companies Acts and financial reporting standards, showing the following notes:

   (i) Accounting policy note for stock and depreciation.

  (ii) Dividends.

 (iii) Interest payable.

 (iv) Operating profit.

  (v) Profit on sale of property.   50

(b) Name the agencies that regulate the production, content and presentation of company financial statements.   10

60 marks

Solution to Question 11.3   50

(a) Profit and Loss Account of Oatfield Plc for the Year Ended 31/12/2010

	Workings	Notes	€
Turnover			1,105,000 ❶
Cost of Sales (75,000 + 696,000 – 77,000 + 8000)		1	702,000 ❼
Gross Profit			403,000
Distribution Cost	W1		50,000 ❷
Administrative Expenses	W2		313,200 ❼ 363,200
			39,800
Other Operating Income			
Discount			6,160 ❶
Operating Profit		2	45,960
Profit on Sale of Land			85,000 ❷
Investment Income			10,800 ❸
			141,760
Interest Payable		3	16,000 ❸
Profit on Ordinary Activities before Taxation ❶			125,760

Taxation			33,000 ❶
Profit after Taxation			92,760
Dividends Paid	4	27,000 ❷	
Dividends Proposed	4	41,000 ❸	68,000
Profit Retained for Year			24,760
Profit Brought Forward at 1/1/2010			73,700 ❶
Profit Carried Forward at 31/12/2010			98,460 ❹

Notes to the Accounts

(i) Accounting Policy Notes ❸

Tangible Fixed Assets

Depreciation is calculated in order to write off the value or cost of tangible fixed assets over their estimated useful economic life, as follows:

Buildings: two per cent per annum – straight-line basis.

Delivery vans: 20 per cent cost.

Stocks: Stocks are valued on a first in, first out basis at the lower of cost and net realisable value.

(ii) Dividends ❹

Ordinary Dividends

Interim Paid 6.0c per Share	21,000	
Final Proposed 10.0c per Share	35,000	56,000
Preference Dividends		
Interim Paid 4.0c per Share	6,000	
Final Proposed 4.0c per Share	6,000	12,000

(iii) Interest Payable ❶

Interest Payable on Debentures Repayable during Years 2016/2017   16,000

(iv) Operating Profit ❸

The operating profit is arrived at after charging:

Depreciation on Tangible Fixed Assets	41,500
Patent Amortised	8,000
Directors' Remuneration	84,000
Auditors' Fees	7,700

(v) Profit on Sale of Property ❶

The company sold land for €85,000 greater than it cost. Cost was €90,000.

Workings

1. Distribution costs		
Advertising	21,000	
Depreciation – Delivery Vans	29,000	50,000
2. Administrative Expenses		
Directors' Fees	84,000	
Salaries and General Expenses	177,000	
Rent	32,000	
Auditors' Fees	7,700	
Depreciation – Buildings	12,500	313,200

(b) 10

Agencies

The Government – Legislation
The European Union – Directives
The Accountancy Profession – FRSs and SSAPs
The Stock Exchange – Listing Rules

12 Costing

aims
- To understand the basic fundamentals of **product and job costing**.
- To be able to **calculate** costing showing all workings.

1. Stock valuation

'Stock should be valued at the lower of **cost** and **net realisable value**,' according to SSAP 9.

'Cost' is the expenditure incurred in bringing the stock to its location and condition. 'Net realisable value' is the estimated selling price less all further costs involved in getting it into saleable condition.

key point

When materials are purchased at different prices during the year, a problem arises as to which price to use when valuing closing stocks. There are different methods, but FIFO is the only one which will be applied. This is also approved under SSAP 9.

2. Overheads and absorption

The **overhead absorption rates** (OAR) to be used will be predetermined, based on machine hours, labour hours, etc.

$$OAR = \frac{\text{Total Overheads of Cost Centre}}{\text{Total Number of Absorption Units}}$$

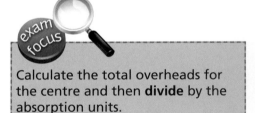

exam focus

Calculate the total overheads for the centre and then **divide** by the absorption units.

3. Apportionment

Where you have non-production departments, the **overheads** of these departments should be apportioned (allocated) among the various production departments. Build up the total overheads of all the departments in the first instance, and then proceed to **eliminate** the service departments among the other departments.

Service Department	Possible Basis of Apportionment
Canteen	Number of Employees
Maintenance	Value of Plant
Stores	Value of Materials
	Frequency of Requisitions

For example, if you have two production departments, a maintenance department and a canteen, the two service departments will be eliminated. Start with the canteen and eliminate its overheads among the two production departments and the maintenance department. Only then eliminate the maintenance department.

Question 12.1

The New Irish Manufacturing Co. Ltd has three separate workshops in one of its factories. The following data relate to this current year:

	Machine Shop	Assembly Shop	Finishing Shop
Direct Labour Hours	14,975	16,343	9,762
Hourly Wage Rates (€)	4.75	4.25	3.75
Variable Factory Overhead (€)	112,312.50	65,372	53,691

Total fixed factory overhead is expected to be €205,400.

A particular customer has requested a piece of specialist equipment, which will require materials from store of 1,000 kg at €4,173 per kilo together with components which will have to be purchased from outside suppliers amounting to €2,457. The packing and delivery costs will amount to €1,151. The following direct labour hours will be required to produce the equipment.

Shop	(hours)
Machine	140
Assembly	160
Finishing	100

Administration cost will be absorbed at 10 per cent of factory cost. For this type of job, it is the company practice to add 20 per cent of the selling price for profit.

You are required to:

Prepare the detailed cost estimate and proposed selling price for this piece of specialist equipment.

Solution to Question 12.1

Specialist Equipment

	Rate	(€)	(€)
Direct Materials			
Materials ex Stores	1,000 kg @ €4.173		4,173
Bought-out Components			2,457
			6,630
Direct Labour			
Machine Shop	140 hr @ €4.75	665	
Assembly Shop	160 hr @ €4.25	680	
Finishing Shop	100 hr @ €3.75	375	1,720

Variable Overhead			
Machine Shop	140 hr @ €7.50	1,050	
Assembly Shop	160 hr @ €4.00	640	
Finishing Shop	100 hr @ €5.50	550	2,240
Fixed Overhead	400 hr @ €5.00		2,000
Factory Cost			12,590
Administration 10% of €12,590			1,259
Packing and Delivery			1,151
Total Cost			15,000
Profit			3,750
Selling Price			18,750

Workings

Rate	(€)	(€)
Variable Overhead Rates		
Machine Shop	$\dfrac{112,321.50}{14,975}$ = 7.50	
Assembly Shop	$\dfrac{65,372}{16,343}$ = 4.00	
Finishing Shop	$\dfrac{53,691}{9,762}$ = 5.50	
Fixed Overhead Rate	$\dfrac{205,400}{14,975 + 16,343 + 9,762}$ = €5.00	

Question 12.2

There are three departments in Timmons Ltd – manufacturing, polishing and packing. For the year 2010, the following are the budgeted costs:

	Total (€)	Manufacturing (€)	Polishing (€)	Packing (€)
Indirect Materials	180,000	110,000	40,000	30,000
Indirect Labour	240,000	120,000	70,000	50,000
Light and Heat	48,000			
Rent and Rates	27,000			
Machine Maintenance	16,000			
Plant Depreciation	80,000			
Factory Canteen	35,000			

The following information relates to the three departments:

	Total	Manufacturing	Polishing	Packing
Floor Space in Square Metres	9,000	4,000	3,000	2,000
Volume in Cubic Metres	24,000	12,000	8,000	4,000
Plant Valuation in € at Book Value	400,000	240,000	100,000	60,000
Machine Hours	60,000	30,000	15,000	15,000
Number of Employees	70	30	30	10
Labour Hours	160,000	80,000	60,000	20,000

Job no. 999 has just been completed. The details are:

	Direct Material	Direct Labour	Machine Hours	Labour Hours
Manufacturing	€7,500	€850	50	20
Polishing	€2,800	€3,900	15	90
Packing	—	€1,500	6	25

The company budgets for a profit margin of 20 per cent of sales.

You are required to:

(a) Calculate the overhead to be absorbed by each department. State clearly the basis of apportionment used.

(b) Calculate a suitable overhead absorption rate for each department.

(c) Compute the selling price of job no. 999.

80 marks

Solution to Question 12.2

31

(a) Overhead Analysis

Overhead	Basis of Apportionment	Total	Manufacturing	Polishing	Packing
Indirect Materials	Actual	180,000	110,000 ❶	40,000 ❶	30,000 ❶
Indirect Labour	Actual	240,000	120,000 ❶	70,000 ❶	50,000 ❶
Light and Heat	Volume ❶	48,000	24,000 ❶	16,000 ❶	8,000 ❶
Rent and Rates	Floor Space ❶	27,000	12,000 ❶	9,000 ❶	6,000 ❶
Machine Maintenance	Machine Hrs ❶	16,000	8,000 ❶	4,000 ❶	4,000 ❶
Plant Depreciation	Plant Valuation ❶	80,000	48,000 ❶	20,000 ❶	12,000 ❶
Factory Canteen	Employees ❶	35,000	15,000 ❶	15,000 ❶	5,000 ❶
		626,000	337,000 ❶	174,000 ❸	115,000 ❶

(b) 21

Overhead Recovery (Absorption) per	Machine Hours Manufacturing	Direct Labour Polishing	Hours Packing
Budgeted Overheads	337,000	174,000	115,000
Budgeted Hours	30,000	60,000	20,000
Overhead Absorption Rate per Machine Hour	€11.23 ❼		
Overhead Absorption Rate per Indirect Labour Hour	€4.21	€2.90 ❼	€5.75 ❼

(c) Selling Price of Job No. 999 28

		€
Direct Materials	(7,500 + 2,800)	10,300.00 ❹
Direct Labour	(850 + 3,900 + 1,500)	6,250.00 ❻
Overheads		
Manufacturing Dept	(50 × €11.23)	561.50 ❺
Polishing Dept	(90 × €290)	261.00 ❺
Packing Dept	(25 × €5.75)	143.75 ❺
Production Cost =	80% of Selling Price	17,516.25
Profit =	20% of Selling Price	4,379.06
Selling Price =	100%	21,895.31 ❸

Question 12.3

(a) Valuation of Closing Stock

The following information relates to the purchases and sales (exclusive of VAT) of O'Leary Ltd for the year 2010.

Period	Details	Quantity and Price
01/01/10 to 31/03/10	Purchases on Credit	4,200 @ €7 each
	Credit Sales	1,300 @ €12 each
	Cash Sales	1,200 @ €11 each
01/04/10 to 30/06/10	Purchases on Credit	3,200 @ €7 each
	Credit Sales	1,350 @ €12 each
	Cash Sales	1,500 @ €12 each

01/07/10 to 30/09/10	Purchases on Credit	2,700 @ €8 each
	Credit Sales	1,400 @ €13 each
	Cash Sales	1,200 @ €11 each
01/10/10 to 31/12/10	Purchases on Credit	3,200 @ €9 each
	Credit Sales	1,600 @ €13 each
	Cash Sales	900 @ €13 each

On 1/1/2010 there was an opening stock of 4,400 units @ €7 each.

You are required to:

(i) Calculate the value of the closing stock, using the first in first out (FIFO) method.

(ii) Prepare a trading account for the year ended 31/12/2010.

(b) Product Costing

O'Mahony Ltd is a small company with three departments. The following are the company's budgeted costs for the coming year:

Department	Variable Costs	Fixed Costs	Wage Rate per Hour
X	€18 per hour	€8.50 per hour	€11
Y	€16 per hour	€7.50 per hour	€12
Z	€20 per hour	€4.00 per hour	€10

General administration overhead absorption rate per hour is budgeted to be €74.50. The following are the specifications for a quotation for job no. 999:

Material costs €6,450.

Labour hours required in each department are:

Department	Hours
X	90
Y	180
Z	50

You are required to:

(i) Calculate the selling price of job no. 999 if the profit is set at 25 per cent of selling price.

(ii) State two reasons for product costing and explain each.

80 marks

Solution to Question 12.3

30

(a) (i)

Purchases in Units		Cost Price	Purchases at Cost €
4,200	@	€7	29,400
3,200	@	€7	22,400
2,700	@	€8	21,600
2,300	@	€9	20,700
12,400			94,100

Sales in Units		Selling Price	Sales Value €
2,400	@	€11	26,400
4,150	@	€12	49,800
3,900	@	€13	50,700
10,450			126,900

Closing Stock in Units	
Opening Stock	4,400
Add Purchases	12,400
	16,800
Less Sales	10,450
Closing Stock	6,350

Closing Stock in €			€
2,300	@	€9	20,700
2,700	@	€8	21,600
1,350	@	€7	9,450
6,350			51,750 ⑮

(ii) Trading Account for Year Ending 31 December 2010

	€	€
Sales		126,900 ❸
Less Cost of Goods Sold		
Opening Stock	30,800 ❷	
Purchases	94,100 ❸	
	124,900	
Less Closing Stock	51,750 ❸	73,150
Gross Profit		53,750 ❹

(b) (i)

50

		€	€
Direct Materials			6,450.00 ❸
Direct Wages			
Department X	(90 hours @ 11)	990 ❸	
Department Y	(180 hours @ 12)	2,160 ❸	
Department Z	(50 hours @ 10)	500 ❸	3,650.00
Variable Overheads			
Department X	(90 hours @ 18)	1,620 ❸	
Department Y	(180 hours @ 16)	2,880 ❸	
Department Z	(50 hours @ 20)	1,000 ❸	5,500.00
Fixed Overheads			
Department X	(90 hours @ 8.50)	765 ❸	
Department Y	(180 hours @ 7.50)	1,350 ❸	
Department Z	(50 hours @ 4.00)	200 ❸	2,315.00
General Administration Overhead (320 hours @ €4.50)			1,400.00 ❹
Total Cost	= 75% of selling price		19,355.00 ❷
Profit	= 25% of selling price		6,451.67
Selling Price	= 100%		25,806.67 ❷

(ii)

- To establish the selling price for the purpose of tendering. ❼
- To control costs – budget versus actual. ❺
- To help planning and decision-making.
- To ascertain the value of closing stock in order to prepare final accounts.

Question 12.4

Roversby Ltd produces a specialised component for the catering industry. The company has two production departments – machinery and assembly – and a service department that maintains the heavy machinery and the air tools used in the assembly section. Budgeted costs for the coming year are as follows:

	€
Rent and Rates	40,000
Insurance of Machinery	25,000
Depreciation of Machinery	440,000
Supervisory Salaries	97,000
Maintenance Supervisor	20,000
Factory Cleaning	18,000
Rubbish Removal Contract	6,000
Lighting and Heating	150,000
Building Insurance	25,000
Indirect Materials	78,000
Maintenance of Fire Prevention Equipment	2,000

The following information is also available:

	Machinery	Assembly	Maintenance
Floor Area (sq m)	4,000	2,500	150
Number of Employees	50	120	6
Value of Machinery (€)	900,000	120,000	

The factory works one seven-hour shift per day in the machinery department and one eight-hour shift per day in the assembly department (48 working weeks).

You are required to:

(a) Prepare an analysis of the overheads showing the basis of allocation and apportionment to the three departments.

(b) Reallocate the maintenance overheads to the production departments.

(c) Calculate an overhead absorption rate based on direct labour hours for each of the two departments.

(d) Calculate the cost of a job which has the following costs:

	Machinery	Assembly
Direct Materials (€)	300	100
Direct Labour (hr)	9	25
Wages Rate (€)	5.50	5.90

Solution to Question 12.4

(a) Roversby Ltd Overheads

	Percentage Apportioned	Machinery	Percentage Apportioned	Assembly	Percentage Apportioned	Maintenance	Total
Floor Area	60	4,000	37.5	2,500	2.5	150	6,650
Employees	28.5	50	68	120	3.5	6	176
Machinery	88	900,000	12	120,000			1,020

Roversby Ltd
(b) Overhead Reallocation

	Machinery (€)	Assembly (€)	Maintenance (€)	Total (€)	Basis
Rent and Rates	24,000	15,000	1,000	40,000	FS
Insurance of Machinery	22,000	3,000		25,000	Value
Depreciation of Machinery	387,200	52,800		440,000	Value
Supervisory Salaries	58,200	36,375	2,425	97,000	FS
Maintenance Supervisor			20,000	20,000	
Factory Cleaning	10,800	6,750	450	18,000	FS
Rubbish Removal Contract	3,600	2,250	150	6,000	FS
Light and Heating	90,000	56,250	3,750	150,000	FS
Building Insurance	15,000	9,375	625	25,000	FS
Indirect Materials	46,800	29,250	1,950	78,000	FS
Maintenance of Fire Prevention Equipment	1,200	750	50	2,000	FS
	658,800	211,800	30,400	901,000	
	26,752	3,648	(30,400)		
	685,552	211,848			

(c)
Machinery
$7 \times 5 \times 48 = 1,680$ hrs; OAR $= 685,552/1,680 = €408.07$
Assembly
$8 \times 5 \times 48 = 1,920$ hrs; OAR $= 211,848/1,920 = €110.34$

(d) Cost of Job

Direct Materials			
Machinery	300		
Assembly	200		400.00
Direct Labour			
Machinery	9 × 5.5	49.50	
Assembly	25 × 5.9	147.50	197.00
Overhead Maintenance	408.07 × 9	3,672.63	
Assembly	110.34 × 25	2,758.50	6,431.13
Budgeted Cost			7,028.13

Question 12.5

Ranelagh Ltd manufactures three products in two production departments, a machine shop and a fitting section; it also has two service departments, a canteen and a machine maintenance section. Shown below are next year's budgeted production data and manufacturing costs for the company:

Product	X	Y	Z
Production (units)	4,200	6,900	1,700
Prime Cost			
Direct Materials (€ Per Unit)	11	14	17
Direct Labour Machine Shop (€ Per Unit)	6	4	2
Fitting Section (€ Per Unit)	12	3	21
Machine Hours (Per Unit)	6	3	4

Budgeted Overheads

	Machine Shop (€)	Fitting Section (€)	Canteen (€)	Machine Maintenance Section (€)	Total (€)
Allocated Overheads	27,660	19,470	16,600	26,650	90,380
Rent, Rates and Light					17,000
Depreciation and Insurance of Equipment					25,000
Additional Data:					
Gross Book Value of Equipment	150,000	75,000	30,000	45,000	
Number of Employees	18	14	4	4	
Floor Space Occupied (sq m)	3,600	1,400	1,000	800	

It has been estimated that approximately 70 per cent of the machine maintenance section's costs are incurred servicing the machine shop and the remainder incurred servicing the fitting section.

You are required to:
(a) Calculate the following overhead absorption rates: a machine hour rate for the machine shop and a rate expressed as a percentage of direct wages for the fitting section. All workings and assumptions should be clearly shown.

(b) Calculate the budgeted manufacturing cost per unit of each product.

Solution to Question 12.5

(a) Overhead Schedule

Expense	Basis of Apportionment	Machine Shop (€)	Fitting Section (€)	Canteen (€)	Machine Maintenance Section (€)	Total (€)
Allocated		27,660	19,470	16,600	26,650	90,380
Rent etc.	Area	9,000	3,500	2,500	2,000	17,000
Depr and Insurance	Book Value	12,500	6,250	2,500	3,750	25,000
		49,160	29,220	21,600	32,400	132,380
Apportionments						
Canteen	Number of Employees	10,800	8,400	(21,600)	2,400	
Maintenance	70 : 30	24,360	10,440		(34,800)	
		84,320	48,060			132,380

Calculation of Total Machine Hours

Product	X	Y	Z	Total
Machine Hours (Per Unit)	6	3	4	
Production (Units)	4,200	6,900	1,700	
Total Machine Hours	25,200	20,700	6,800	52,700

Total overhead apportioned to the machine shop is €84,320. Therefore, the absorption rate per machine hour is €1.60.

Calculation of Payroll Total for Fitting Section

Product	X	Y	Z	Total
Wages (€ Per Unit)	12	3	21	
Production (Units)	4,200	6,900	1,700	
Payroll Total (€)	50,400	20,700	35,600	106,800

Total overhead apportioned to the fitting section is €48,060. Therefore, the absorption rate as a percentage of direct wages is $48,050/106,800 \times 100 = 45\%$.

(b) Cost of Production (per unit)

	(€)	X (€)	(€)	Y (€)	(€)	Z (€)
Prime Cost						
Direct Materials		11		14		17
Direct Labour – Machine Shop		6		4		2
Direct Labour – Fitting Section		12		3		21
		29		21		40
Overhead						
Machine Shop (per Machine Hr)	9.6		4.80		6.40	
Fitting Section (per Direct Wages)	5.4		1.35		9.45	
		15		6.15		15.85
Cost of Production		44		27.15		55.85

Question 12.6

A picture-framing firm had the following transactions for the six months ended 31 December 2010. The figures are exclusive of VAT.

Purchases		Sales	
2010		**2010**	
25 July	Purchased 150 units @ €20 each	15 Sept	Sold 305 units @ €45 each
28 Aug	Purchased 225 units @ €30 each	4 Oct	Sold 50 units @ €45 each
10 Nov	Purchased 410 units @ €40 each	23 Dec	Sold 100 units @ €75 each

Additional information:

1. The balance sheet at 1 July 2010 was as follows:

   Bank Balance   €10,000

   Capital Account   €10,000
2. Two months' credit is taken from suppliers.
3. One month's credit is given to debtors.
4. Expenses of €1,400 are paid each month as incurred.
5. Assume that purchases are liable to VAT at 10 per cent. Assume that sales are liable to VAT at 20 per cent.

You are required to:

(a) Calculate the value of closing stock at the end of each month during the period 1 July 2010 to 31 December 2010, using the first in, first out (FIFO) method.
(b) Prepare the trading and profit and loss accounts and balance sheet for the six months ended 31 December 2010 and the balance sheet at that date.

Solution to Question 12.6

(a) Stock Valuation – FIFO

Date 2010	Purchases			Sales			Balance	
	Units	**€**	**Total**	**Units**	**€**	**Total**	**Units**	**Total**
25 July	150	20	3,000				150	3,000
28 Aug	225	30	6,750				375	9,750
15 Sept				305				
				150	20	3,000		
				155	30	4,650	70	2,100

				50	30	1,500	20	600
4 Oct				50	30	1,500	20	600
10 Nov	410	40	16,400				430	17,000
23 Dec				100				
				20	30	600		
				80	40	3,200	330	13,200

(b) Trading and Profit and Loss Accounts for Six Months Ended 31 December 2010

	(€)	(€)
Sales		223,475
Less Costs Purchases	26,150	
Closing Stock	13,200	
Cost		12,950
Gross Profit		10,525
Less Expenses		8,400
Net Profit		72,125

Balance Sheet at 31 December 2010

	(€)	(€)
Current Assets		
Stock	13,200	
Debtors (100 × 75 + 20%)	9,000	
Bank	7,825	
VAT Refund Due	140	
	30,165	
Less Current Liabilities		
Creditors (410 × 40 + 10%)	(18,040)	12,125
Financed by		
Capital	10,000	
Plus Net Profit	2,125	
		12,125

13 Marginal Costing

When doing Higher Level questions on this topic, adopt the following steps:

1. Find the number of units involved.
2. Find the selling price per unit.
3. Find the variable cost per unit.
4. Find the contribution per unit. This is selling price − variable cost.
5. Find the total fixed costs.
6. Find the break-even units. This is fixed costs/contribution.
7. Find the margin of safety. This is units sold − break-even units.

The information gained in these seven steps will allow you to answer any question involving marginal costing.

Use the following simple formula every time

$$\text{Selling Price} - \text{Variable Costs} = \text{Contribution (per unit)}$$
$$\text{Contribution} \times \text{Units Sold} = \text{Total Contribution}$$
$$\text{Total Contribution} - \text{Fixed Costs} = \text{Profit}$$
$$\frac{\text{Fixed Costs}}{\text{Contribution (per unit)}} = \text{Breakeven}$$
$$\frac{\text{Contribution}}{\text{Sales Price}} = \text{Contribution Sales Ratio}$$

Break-even charts

There are different acceptable methods by which break-even charts may be drawn up. The one shown here could be referred to as the 'traditional method':

1. Draw the X and Y axes. The X, or horizontal, axis is for units, and the Y, or vertical, axis is for monetary values.

2. Draw the fixed costs as a straight line parallel to the X axis.

3. Next draw the total costs line as a straight but sloping line, with the slope depending on the level of variable costs. (Note that you do not draw the variable costs as a separate line; rather they are the difference between fixed and total costs.)

4. Then draw the sales/revenue line as a straight/sloping line from the origin.

5. Where the sales line intersects the total costs line is the break-even point.

6. The section above this represents profit and the section below loss.

Example

A company makes a product with a maximum capacity of €500,000 per annum. The unit selling price is €1, and the variable costs are €0.60 per unit. The fixed costs are €120,000. Draw a break-even chart showing the profit at the projected sales/production level of 400,000.

$$\text{Selling Price} = 1.00$$
$$\text{Variable Costs} = 0.60$$
$$= \overline{\qquad}$$
$$\text{Contribution} = 0.40$$
$$\text{Break-even} = \frac{120,000}{0.40}$$
$$= 3,000,000 \text{ units}$$

Question 13.1

You work as a product accountant for Gene's Jeans and are working on the planned estimates for the next year of one of your company's products. The following are the budgeted costs of producing 12,000 units:

	€
Direct Labour	156,000
Direct Material	228,000
Production Overheads:	
Indirect Labour	24,000
Indirect Expenses	66,000
Administration Overheads	246,000
	720,000

You also have the following information:

1. The maximum possible capacity is for 14,000 units.

2. To obtain the selling price, a mark-up of 25 per cent is used.

3. Your research into cost behaviour reveals that:
   (a) Indirect labour is 10 per cent variable.
   (b) Indirect expenses are estimated to be €3.60 per unit variable with the balance being fixed.

(c) Direct labour and direct material are 100 per cent variable.

(d) All other costs are considered fixed.

You are required to:

(a) Prepare a suitable table to show fixed and variable costs based on an output of 12,000 units.

(b) Calculate:

(i) The selling price.

(ii) The contribution per unit.

(iii) The break-even point in units.

(c) Prepare a break-even chart based on 12,000 units of output, clearly indicating:

(i) Area of loss.

(ii) Area of profit.

(iii) Margin of safety.

(d) If the price were reduced by five per cent, output/sales would rise to 14,000 units. What would the profit be?

Solution to Question 13.1

Gene's Jeans
(a) Table of Costs

	Variable (€)	Fixed (€)	Total (€)
Direct Labour	156,000		156,000
Direct Material	228,000		228,000
Indirect Labour	2,400	21,600	24,000
Indirect Expenses	43,200	22,800	66,000
Administration Expenses	_____	246,000	246,000
	429,600	290,400	720,000

(b)(i)

$$\text{Total Costs} = €20,000$$

$$\text{Unit Costs} = \frac{720,000}{12,000} = €60$$

Selling Price = Cost + 25% = 60 + 15 = €75.

(ii)

Contribution per Unit = Selling Price − Variable Costs

	(€)	(€)
Selling Price		75.00
Variable Costs		
Direct Labour	13.00	
Direct Material	19.00	
Indirect Labour	0.20	
Indirect Expenses	3.60	35.80
Contribution		39.20

(iii)

$$\text{Break-even} = \frac{\text{Fixed Cost}}{\text{Contribution per Unit}}$$

$$= \frac{290,400}{39.20} = 7,408 \text{ Units}$$

(c)

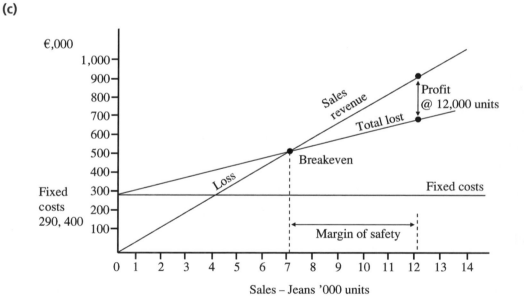

(d)

$$\text{Selling Price} - 5\% = \text{Units Sold}$$
$$\text{Selling Price} = 75 - 5\% = 71.25$$
$$\text{Less Variable Costs} = \underline{35.80}$$
$$\text{Contribution} = 35.45$$
$$\text{Total Contribution} = 35.45 \times 14{,}000 = 496{,}300$$
$$\text{Profit} = \text{Total Contribution} - \text{Fixed Costs}$$
$$205{,}900 = 496{,}300 - 290{,}400$$
$$\text{Profit @ 12{,}000 Units} = (39.20 \times 12{,}000) - 290{,}400 = 180{,}000$$

Question 13.2

O'Connor produces a single product. The company's profit and loss account for the year ended 31/12/2010, during which 80,000 units were produced and sold, was as follows:

	€	€
Sales		960,000
Materials	320,000	
Labour	200,000	
Factory Overheads	120,000	
Administration Expenses	110,000	
Selling Expenses	90,000	
		840,000
Net Profit		120,000

The materials, labour and 60 per cent of the factory overheads are variable costs. Apart from the sale of five per cent of sales, selling and administration expenses are fixed.

You are required to calculate:

(a) The company's break-even point and margin of safety.

(b) The number of units that must be sold in 2011 if the company is to increase its net profit by 20 per cent over the 2010 figure, assuming the selling price and cost levels and percentages remain unchanged.

(c) The profit the company would make in 2011 if it reduced its selling price to €11, increased fixed costs by €13,000 and thereby increased the number of units sold to 100,000, with all other cost levels and percentages remaining unchanged.

(d) The selling price the company must charge in 2011, if fixed costs are increased by 10 per cent but the volume of sales and the profit remain the same.

(e) The number of units that must be sold at €13 per unit to provide a profit of 10 per cent of the sales revenue from these same units.

(f) Explain two limitations of marginal costing.

Solution to Question 13.2

O'Connor Solution

80,000 units   Selling Price = 960,000/80,000 = €12 Per Unit

Costs	Total	Fixed	Variable	Var. Per Unit
Materials	320,000	–	320,000	4.00
Labour	200,000	–	200,000	2.50
Factory Overheads	120,000	48,000	72,000	0.90
Administration	110,000	110,000	–	
Selling	90,000	42,000	48,000	0.60
	840,000	200,000	640,000	8.00

Contribution = 1200 − 8.00 = 4.00

(a)

$$\text{Break-even} = 200,000/4 = 50,000 \text{ Units}$$
$$\text{Margin of Safety} = 80,000 - 50,000 = 30,000 \text{ Units}$$

(b)

$$\text{Selling Price} = 12.00$$
$$\text{Variable Cost} = 8.00$$
$$\text{Contribution} = 4.00$$
$$\text{Total Contribution} = 4 \times X = ?$$
$$\text{Fixed Costs} = 200,000$$
$$\text{Profit} = 120,000 + 20\% = 144,000$$
$$\text{Therefore } (200,000 + 144,000)/4 = 86,000 \text{ Units}$$

(c)

$$\text{Selling Price} = 11.00$$
$$\text{Variable Cost} = 7.95 \text{ (selling exs} = 0.550)$$
$$\text{Contribution} = 3.05$$
$$\text{Total Contribution} = 3.05 \times 100,000 = 305,000$$
$$\text{Fixed Costs} = 200,000 + 13,000 = 213,000$$
$$\text{Profit} = 92,000$$

(d)

Selling Price   = X

Variable Costs

Materials   4.00

Labour   2.50

Factory Overheads .90

Selling   5%X

Therefore Contribution		= Y	
Total Contribution		= Y × 80,000	= ?
Fixed Costs		= 200,000 = 10%	= 220,000
Profit			= 120,000
Therefore	(220,000 + 120,000)/80,000		= 4.25 = Y (Contribution)
Selling Price	– Variable Cost		= Contribution
X	– 4.00 – 2.50 – 0.90 – 1/20 X		= 4.25
19/20 X	= 4.25 + 4.00 + 2.50 + 0.90		= 11.65
		X	= 12.26

(e)

$$\text{Formula} = \text{Fixed Costs}/(\text{Contribution} - 10\% \times \text{Selling Price})$$
$$= 200,000/(4.95 - 1.30)$$
$$= 54,795 \text{ Units}$$

Note: Required selling price is €13.00.
Selling expenses become 0.65 per unit and contribution = €4.95.

(f)

Limitations of marginal costing:

1. Assumes that all stock is sold. Production = sales.
2. Assumes that all costs behave in a linear fashion through all stages. This is unrealistic. Fixed costs will be stepped, fixed and variable may increase or reduce per unit. Quantity stock discounts may be obtained and labour cost may increase through overtime.

Question 13.3

Quigley Ltd produces a single product. The company's profit and loss account for the year ended 31/12/2010 during which 70,000 units were produced and sold, was as follows:

	€	€
Sales		910,000
Materials	315,000	
Direct Labour	175,000	
Factory Overheads	63,000	
Administration Expenses	105,000	
Selling Expenses	85,000	743,000
Net Profit		167,000

The materials, direct labour and 40 per cent of the factory overheads are variable costs. Apart from sales commission of five per cent of sales, selling and administration expenses are fixed.

You are required to calculate:

(a) The company's break-even and margin of safety.

(b) The number of units that must be sold in 2011 if the company is to increase its net profit by 20 per cent over the 2010 figure, assuming the selling price and cost levels and percentages remain unchanged.

(c) The profit the company would make in 2011 if it reduced its selling price to €12, increased fixed costs by €11,000 and thereby increased the number of units sold to 85,000, with all other cost levels and percentages remaining unchanged.

(d) The selling price the company must charge per unit in 2011, if fixed costs are increased by 10 per cent but the volume of sales and the profit remain the same.

(e) The number of units that must be sold at €14 per unit to provide a profit of 10 per cent of the sales revenue from these same units.

Solution to Question 13.3

Costs	Total	Fixed	Variable	Var. per unit
Materials	315,000	–	315,000	4.50
Direct Labour	175,000	–	175,000	2.50
Factory Overheads	63,000	37,800	25,200	0.36
Administration	105,000	105,000	–	–
Selling Expenses	85,000	39,500	45,500	0.65
	743,000	182,300	560,700	8.01

Contribution = Selling Price − Variable Cost
$$= 13.00 - 8.01 = 4.99$$

(a)   Break-even Point = Fixed Costs/Contribution

$$= \frac{182,300}{4.99} = 36,534 \text{ Units}$$

Margin of Safety = Sales Units − Break-even Units
$$= 70,000 - 36,534 = 33,466 \text{ Units}$$

(b)   Selling Price = 13.00

Less Variable Cost = 8.01

Contribution = 4.99

Total Contribution = 4.99 × X =

Less Fixed Costs = 182,300

Profit = 167,000 + 20% = 200,400

$$\text{Therefore} = \frac{182,300 + 200,400}{4.99} = X = 76,694 \text{ Units}$$

(c)   Selling Price = 12.00

Less Variable Cost 8.01 − 0.05 = 7.96

Contribution = 4.04

Total Contribution =   4.04 × 85,000 = 343,400

Less Fixed Costs = 182,300 + 11,000 = 193,300

Profit   = 150,100

(d)

$$\text{Selling Price} \quad = X$$

Less Variable Cost

Material	$= 4.50$
Labour	$= 2.50$
Overheads	$= 0.36$
Selling	$= 1/20X$

$$\text{Contribution} = Y$$

$$\text{Total Contribution} = Y \times 70,000 \quad =$$

$$\text{Less Fixed Costs} = 182,300 + 10\% = \underline{200,530}$$

$$\text{Profit} = 167,000$$

$$\text{Therefore } \frac{200,530 + 167,000}{70,000} = Y = 5.25$$

$$\text{Therefore } X - 4.50 - 2.50 - 0.36 - 1/20X = 5.25$$

$$19/20X = 4.50 + 2.50 + 0.36 + 5.25 \quad = 12.61$$

$$\text{Therefore X ie Selling Price} = 13.27$$

(e)

Selling Price	$= 14.00$
Less Variable Cost	$= \underline{8.06}$
Contribution	5.94

$$\frac{\text{Fixed Costs}}{\text{Contribution} - 10\% \text{ S.P.}} = \frac{182,300}{5.94 - 1.40} = 40,155 \text{ Units}$$

Question 13.4

Murphy Ltd produces a single product. The company's profit and loss account for the year ended 31/12/2010, during which 60,000 were produced and sold, was as follows:

	€	€
Sales (60,000 units)		960,000
Materials	360,000	
Direct Labour	156,000	
Factory Overheads	81,000	
Administration Expenses	106,000	
Selling Expenses	65,000	768,000
Net Profit		192,000

The materials, direct labour and 40 per cent of the factory overheads are variable costs. Apart from the sales commission of €0.60 per unit, selling and administration expenses are fixed.

You are required to calculate:

(a) The company's break-even and margin of safety.

(b) The number of units that must be sold in 2011 if the company is to increase its net profit by 20 per cent over the 2010 figure, assuming the selling price and cost levels and percentages remain unchanged.

(c) The profit the company would make in 2011 if it reduced its selling price to €15, increased fixed costs by €16,000 and thereby increased the number of units sold to 76,000, with all other cost levels and percentages remaining unchanged.

(d) The selling price the company must charge in 2011, if fixed costs increase by 10 per cent but the volume of sales and the profit remain the same.

(e) The number of units that must be sold at €17 per unit to provide a profit of 10 per cent of the sales revenue from these same units.

(f) List and explain two limitations/assumptions of marginal costing.

Solution to Question 13.4

$$\text{Selling Price} = \frac{960,000}{60,000} = 16.00$$

Costs	Total	Fixed	Variable	Var. p.u.
Materials	360,000	–	360,000	6.00
Direct Labour	156,000	–	156,000	2.60
Factory Overheads	81,000	48,600	32,400	0.54
Administration	106,000	106,000	–	–
Selling	65,000	29,000	36,000	0.60
	768,000	183,600	584,400	9.74

Contribution $= 16.00 - 9.74 = 6.26$

(a) $\text{Break-even} = \dfrac{\text{Fixed Costs}}{\text{Contribution}} = \dfrac{183,600}{6.26} = 29,330 \text{ Units}$

Margin of Safety $=$ Sales Units $-$ Break-even Units

$= 60,000 - 29,330 \qquad = 30,670 \text{ Units}$

(b)   Selling Price $= 16.00$

Less Variable Cost $= 9.74$

Contribution $= 6.26$

Total Contribution $= 6.26 \times X =$

Less Fixed Costs $= 183,600$

Profit $192,000 + 20\% = 230,400$

Therefore $\dfrac{183,600 + 230,400}{6.26} = 66,135 \text{ Units}$

(c)
$$\text{Selling Price} = 15.00$$
$$\text{Less Variable Cost} = \underline{9.74}$$
$$\text{Contribution} = 5.26$$
$$\text{Total Contribution} = 5.26 \times 76,000 \ = 399,760$$
$$\text{Less Fixed Costs} = 183,600 + 16,000 = \underline{199,600}$$
$$\text{Net Profit} \qquad\qquad\qquad\qquad 200,160$$

(d)
$$\text{Selling Price} = X$$
$$\text{Less Variable Cost} = 9.74$$
$$\text{Contribution} = Y$$

Total Contribution $= Y \times 60,000 =$

Less Fixed Costs $= 183,600 + 10\% = 201,960$

Net Profit $= 192,000$

$$\text{Therefore } 201,960 + 192,000 \div 60,000 = 6.57 = Y$$
$$X - 9.74 = 6.57$$
$$X \text{ i.e. Selling price} = 16.31$$

(e) $\dfrac{\text{Fixed Costs}}{\text{Contribution} - 10\% \text{ of SP}} = \dfrac{183,600}{7.26 - 1.60} = 33,022 \text{ Units}$

(f)

1. Marginal costing assumes that production = sales, thus ignoring closing stock. This is not so.
2. Marginal costing assumes that the selling price remains constant at all levels, ignoring such things as quantity discounts and special sales price reductions.
3. Marginal costing is a very useful tool in short-term decision-making.

Extra theory question

Compare marginal costing and absorption costing.

1. Marginal costing uses the concept of the contribution. This is not used in absorption costing. The contribution is a great aid to planning and decision-making.
2. In preparing financial final accounts, absorption costing must be used in line with statements of standard accounting practice.
3. Closing stocks are valued higher using absorption costing because a portion of the fixed costs is included.

14 Budgets

aims

- To be able to prepare the different forms of budgets – **production, cash** and **flexible budgets**.
- To be able to **analyse** properly these prepared budgets.

Subsidiary budgets

$$\text{Sales Budget} = \text{Budgeted Unit Sales} \times \text{Budgeted Selling Price}$$

$$\text{Production Budget} = \text{Budgeted Sales} + \text{Budgeted Closing Stock} - \text{Budgeted Opening Stock}$$

$$\text{Materials Usage Budget} = \text{Production Units} \times \text{Units of Different Materials Required per Product}$$

$$\text{Materials Purchase Budget} = \text{Materials Usage Budget} + \text{Closing Stock of Materials} - \text{Opening Stock of Materials}$$

key point

To answer questions about budgets you need to know how to both prepare and analyse all three different types of budget.

Principal budgets

There are three principal budgets:

1. Cash budget
2. Budgeted profit and loss account
3. Budgeted balance sheet.

Great care needs to be taken in drawing up these budgets. An examination, done a year later, of business start-up plans submitted to financial institutions revealed that over 90 per cent were seriously in error. Sales and the ability to collect had been seriously overestimated. Cost of sales and the ability to obtain credit had been seriously under- and overestimated. The amount of various expenses had been underestimated. This has been identified as a major cause of new business failure.

exam TIPS

1 **Cash budgets**

(a) Remember, only actual receipts and payments are included.

(b) These are included when actually received and paid, not when due.

(c) Depreciation is always excluded (non-cash item).

(d) Credit sales and purchases at end of period are excluded.

(e) Changes in stock levels will affect cash budgets.

(f) The closing balance at end of period one is equal to the opening balance at beginning of period two.

2 **Budgeted profit and loss account**

(a) If you are using a total column in your cash budget, the total figure does not necessarily become the profit and loss figure.

(b) Include all sales/purchases, i.e. both cash and credit, for the period.

(c) Exclude accruals at the beginning and pre-payments at the end of the period.

(d) Include depreciation.

(**Note:** Many budgets are for six months, and the depreciation will be per annum, so remember to allocate properly.)

(e) Exclude capital expenditure.

3 **Budgeted balance sheet**

(a) Include the total of all fixed assets and the relevant depreciation.

(b) Ensure that you calculate the closing stock figure at the cost price, not the selling price.

(c) Debtors = unpaid credit sales.

(d) The cash figure is the closing cash figure from your cash budget.

(e) Creditors = unpaid credit purchases.

(f) Include accruals and pre-payments at the period end.

Question 14.1

O'Reilly manufactures a component for the electronics industry. The following flexible budgets have already been prepared for 55 per cent, 70 per cent and 85 per cent of the plant's capacity:

Output Levels	55%	70%	85%
Units	11,000	14,000	17,000
Cost	€	€	€
Direct Materials	143,000	182,000	221,000
Direct Wages	99,000	126,000	153,000
Production Overheads	74,000	92,000	110,000
Other Overhead Costs	36,000	45,000	54,000
Administration Expenses	29,000	29,000	29,000
	381,000	474,000	567,000

Profit is budgeted to be 22 per cent of sales.

You are required to:
(a) (i) Classify the above costs into fixed, variable and mixed costs.
  (ii) Separate production overheads into fixed and variable elements.
  (iii) Separate other overhead costs into fixed and variable elements.
  (iv) Prepare a flexible budget for 96 per cent activity level.
  (v) Restate the budget using marginal costing principles and show the contribution.
(b) Explain principal budget factor. Why prepare a flexible budget and what does it show?

80 marks

Solution to Question 14.1

80

(a) (i) Direct Materials ❶ Variable
  Direct Wages ❶ Variable
  Production Overheads ❷ Mixed
  Other Overhead Costs ❷ Mixed
  Administration Expenses ❷ Mixed

(ii) Production overheads

	Units €	Total Cost €
High	17,000	110,000
Low	11,000	74,000
Difference	6,000	36,000

The variable cost of 6,000 units is €36,000, therefore the variable cost per unit is €6. ❻

	€ 55%	€ 70%	€ 85%
Total Production Overhead Cost	74,000	92,000	110,000
Variable Cost (Units × 76)	66,000	84,000	102,000
Therefore Fixed Cost	8,000	8,000	8,000 ❻

(iii) Other overhead costs

	Units €	Total Cost €
High	17,000	54,000
Low	11,000	36,000
Difference	6,000	18,000

The variable cost of 6,000 units is €18,000, therefore the variable cost per unit is €3. ❻

	€ 55%	€ 70%	€ 85%
Total Other Overhead Costs at	36,000	45,000	54,000
Variable Cost (Units × 73)	33,000	42,000	51,000
Therefore, Fixed Cost	3,000	3,000	3,000 ❻

(iv) Production overheads at the required flexible budgeted level of 96 per cent – (19,200 units)

	€
Variable Cost (19,200 Units × 769)	115,200
Fixed Cost	8,000
Total Cost	123,200 *

Other overhead costs at the required flexible budgeted level of 96 per cent – (19,200 units)

	€
Variable Cost (19,200 Units × 73)	57,600
Fixed Cost	3,000
Total Cost	60,600 *

Construction of a flexible budget for a 96 per cent activity level

		Flexible Budget
Activity Level		96%
Units		19,200
		€
Direct Materials	(€13 × 19,200)	249,600 ❸
Direct Wages	(€9 × 19,200)	172,800 ❸
Production Overheads	(€6 × 19,200) + 8,000	*123,200 ❻
Administration Overheads (Fixed)		29,000 ❷
Other Overhead Costs	(€3 × 19,200) + 3,000	*60,600 ❻
Total Cost (78% of Sales)		635,200

(v) Flexible budget in marginal costing format

	€	€
Sales		814,359 ❶
Less Variable Costs		
Direct Materials	249,600 ❶	
Direct Wages	172,800 ❶	
Variable Production Costs	115,200 ❶	
Other Overhead Costs	57,600 ❶	595,200
Contribution ❶		219,159
Less Fixed Costs		
Production Costs	8,000 ❶	
Selling and Distribution Costs	3,000 ❶	
Administration Costs	29,000 ❶	40,000
Profit		179,159 ❸

(b)
Principal budget factor – Often referred to as the limiting budget factor or the key budget factor. ❼
This is the factor that limits output and therefore prevents continuous expansion. Usually the principal budget factor is sales demand. The principal budget factor could be some other limiting factor such as availability of materials.
Why prepare a flexible budget and what does it show?
- To compare budgeted costs and actual costs at the same level of activity. ❻
- To compare like with like.
- To help in controlling costs or to plan product levels.
- They show whether actual costs exceeded or were less than budgeted costs (variances). ❸

Question 14.2

O'Toole had the following assets and liabilities at 1 January 2010:

	€	€
Assets		
Stock	47,250	
Debtors	8,000	
Cash	1,500	
Rates Prepaid (3 Months)	600	57,350
Liabilities		
Capital		57,350

O'Toole expects the sales for the next seven months will be as follows:

Jan	Feb	March	April	May	June	July
€63,000	€81,000	€75,000	€69,000	€72,000	€75,000	€87,000

1. 80 per cent of sales are for cash and 20 per cent are on credit, collected one month after sale.
2. Gross profit as percentage of sales is 25 per cent.
3. O'Toole wishes to keep a minimum cash balance of €6,000 at the end of each month.
4. All borrowings are in multiples of a thousand euro and interest is at the rate of 10 per cent per annum.
5. Purchases each month should be sufficient to cover the following month's sales.
6. Purchases are paid for by the end of the month.
7. Purchased machine on 1 February for €12,000 (depreciation 15 per cent per annum on cost).
8. O'Toole rents the premises for €24,000 per annum, payable each month.
9. Wages amounting to €12,500 are paid each month.
10. Purchased for cash on 1 April a computer for €2,200 (depreciation of 20 per cent per annum on cost).
11. Rates paid for six months from 1 April were €2,400 (paid in April).
12. One-quarter of the money borrowed on 31/1/2010 is to be repaid at the end of June, together with interest to date on the repaid amount.

You are required to prepare a:

(a) Cash budget for the six-month period from January to June.
(b) Budgeted profit and loss (pro-forma income statement) for the six months ended 30/6/2010.

80 marks

60

Solution to Question 14.2

(a) Cash Budget (Forecast) January/June

	Jan €	Feb €	Mar €	April €	May €	June €
Receipts						
Cash Sales Receipts	50,400 ①	64,800 ①	60,000 ①	55,200 ①	57,600 ①	60,000 ①
Credit Sales Receipts						
One Month	8,000 ②	12,600 ①	16,200 ①	15,000 ①	13,800 ①	14,400 ①
	58,400	77,400	76,200	70,200	71,400	74,400
Payments						
Machinery		12,000 ①				
Purchases – Materials	60,750 ②	56,250 ②	51,750 ②	54,000 ②	56,250 ②	65,250 ②
Rent	2,000 ①	2,000 ①	2,000 ①	2,000 ①	2,000 ①	2,000 ①
Computer				2,200 ①		
Rates				2,400 ①		
Loan Repayment and Interest						5,729 ③
Wages/Labour	12,500 ①	12,500 ①	12,500 ①	12,500 ①	12,500 ①	12,500 ①
	75,250	82,750	66,250	73,100	70,750	85,479
Net Monthly Cash Flow	(16,850) ①	(5,350) ①	9,950 ①	(2,900) ①	650 ①	(11,079) ①
Bank Loan – Financing (3)	22,000 ①	5,000 ①				
Opening Balance	1,500 ①	6,650	6,300	16,250	13,350	4,000 ①
Closing Balance	6,650	6,300	16,250	13,350	14,000	6,921 ④

(b) Budgeted Income Statement for Six Months Ended 30/6/2010 20

	€	€
Sales:		435,000 ❶
Less Cost of Sales (75% of €435,000)		
Opening Stock	47,250.00 ❶	
Purchases	344,250.00 ❶	
	391,500.00	
Less Closing Stock (75% of July sales)	65,250.00 ❶	326,250.00
Gross Profit		108,750.00
Less Expenses		
Wages	75,000.00 ❶	
Rent	12,000.00 ❶	
Rates less Prepaid	1,800.00 ❹	
Interest	1,084.00 ❺	
Depreciation – Machinery	750.00 ❷	
– Computer	110.00 ❷	90,744.00
Profit		18,006.00 ❸

Workings

W1 Interest	€5,500 for 5 months at 10% =	229
W2 Interest	€22,000 for 5 months at 10% = 917	
	5,000 for 4 months at 10% = 167	1,084

Question 14.3

Quinlan Ltd has recently completed its sales forecasts for the year to 31 December 2010. It expects to sell two products – Primary at €190 and Superb at €230. All stocks are to be reduced by 20 per cent from their opening levels by the end of 2010 and are valued using the FIFO method.

	Primary	**Superb**
Sales demand is expected to be:	6,000 units	4,500 units

Stocks of finished goods on 1 January 2010 are expected to be:

Primary	350 units @ €160.00 each
Superb	250 units @ €180.00 each

Both products use the same raw materials and skilled labour but in different quantities per unit, as follows:

	Primary	Superb
Material W	6 kg	5 kg
Material X	4 kg	7 kg
Skilled labour	7 hours	8 hours

Stocks of raw materials on 1 January 2010 are expected to be:

Material W	5,000 kg @ €2.50 per kg
Material X	4,000 kg @ €4.50 per kg

The expected prices for raw materials during 2010 are:

Material W	€3 per kg
Material X	€5 per kg

The skilled labour rate is expected to be €11.00 per hour.

The company's production overhead costs are expected to be:

Variable	€4.50 per skilled labour hour
Fixed	€116,000 per annum

You are required to prepare, for the year to 31 December 2010, Quinlan Ltd's:

(a) Production budget (in units).

(b) Raw material purchases budget (in units and €).

(c) Production cost/manufacturing budget.

(d) Budgeted trading account (*if the budgeted cost of a unit of Primary and Superb is €157 and €186, respectively*).

`80 marks`

Solution to Question 14.3

(a) Production Budget

	Primary	Superb
Sales	6,000	4,500
Closing Stock	280	200
Less Opening Stock	350	250
Production	5,930	4,450

(b) Raw Materials Budget

		Mat W	Mat X
Primary	5,930 × 6	35,580	
	5,930 × 4		23,720
Superb	4,450 × 5	22,250	
	4,450 × 7		31,150
Material Usage		57,830	54,870
Closing Stock		4,000	3,200
Less Opening Stock		5,000	4,000
		56,830	54,070
× Purchase Price		× 3	× 5
		170,490	270,350
		€440,840	

(c) Manufacturing Budget

Raw Materials	30,500	
Purchases	440,840	
Less Closing Stock	28,000	
Cost of Raw Materials		433,340
Wages		848,210
Variable Overheads		346,995
Fixed Overheads		116,000
Cost of Production		1,754,545

(d) Budgeted Trading Account

Sales		2,175,000
Less Cost		
Opening Stock	101,000	
Plus Production	1,754,545	
Less Closing Stock	81,160	
Cost of Sales		1,774,385
Gross Profit		400,615

Question 14.4

A friend of yours, C. Priestly, is thinking of setting up in business and has drawn up the following plans:

1. On 1 September 2010 Priestly plans to deposit €120,000 in a business bank account.
2. On 2 September 2010 Priestly plans to buy and pay for premises with €70,000.
3. On 3 September 2010 he plans to buy other fixed assets for €50,000, half of which is to be paid in September and the other half in December.
4. He plans to employ two sales assistants whose monthly wages amount to €1,300, payable at the end of each month (ignore tax and insurance).
5. He plans to sell the following goods.

	Sept	Oct	Nov	Dec	Jan	Feb
Units	450	550	600	600	750	800

Units will be sold on a credit basis for €50 each, and debtors are expected to settle their accounts two months after the month in which goods are sold.

6. He plans to buy the following goods.

	Sept	Oct	Nov	Dec	Jan	Feb
Units	1,000	500	500	600	700	800

Units will cost €20 each, and suppliers expect to be paid in the month following the month in which the goods are bought.

7. Other expenses are estimated at €850 per month payable one month in arrears.
8. Priestly expects to make monthly cash drawings of €1,500.
9. All assets, other than premises, are to be depreciated at the rate of 10 per cent per annum. Premises are to be depreciated at the rate of five per cent per annum.

You are required to:

(a) Prepare the schedule of payments for the six months ending February 2011.
(b) Prepare the cash budget for the six months ending February 2011.
(c) Prepare the budgeted trading and profit and loss accounts and balance sheet for the period ending 28 February 2011.

Solution to Question 14.4

(a) Sales Budget

	Sept	Oct	Nov	Dec	Jan	Feb
Units	450	550	600	600	750	800
Total (€)	22,500	27,500	30,000	30,000	37,500	40,000
Receipts (€)			22,500	27,500	30,000	30,000

Purchases Budget

	Sept	Oct	Nov	Dec	Jan	Feb
Units	1,000	500	500	600	700	800
Total (€)	20,000	10,000	10,000	12,000	14,000	16,000
		20,000	10,000	12,000	12,000	14,000

(b) Cash Budget

	Sept	Oct	Nov	Dec	Jan	Feb	Total
Inflows							
Sales (€)			22,500	27,500	30,000	30,000	110,000
Outflows							
Purchases (€)		20,000	10,000	10,000	12,000	14,000	66,000
Premises (€)	70,000						70,000
Fixed Assets (€)	25,000			25,000			50,000
Wages (€)	1,300	1,300	1,300	1,300	1,300	1,300	7,800
General Expenses (€)		850	850	850	850	850	4,250
Drawings (€)	1,500	1,500	1,500	1,500	1,500	1,500	9,000
	97,800	23,650	13,650	38,650	15,650	17,650	207,050
Opening Balance (€)	120,000	22,200	(1,450)	7,400	(3,750)	10,600	120,000
Net Cash (€)	(97,800)	(23,650)	8,850	(11,150)	14,350	12,350	(97,050)
Closing Balance (€)	22,200	(1,450)	7,400	(3,750)	10,600	22,950	22,950

(c) Trading and Profit and Loss Accounts

	(€)	(€)	(€)
Sales (3,750 × 50)			187,500
Less Costs			
Opening Stock			
Purchases (4,100 × 20)		82,000	
Closing Stock (350 × 20)		7,000	
Cost of Sales			75,000
Gross Profit			112,500
Less Expenses			
Wages		7,800	
Sundries (850 × 6)		5,100	
Depreciation: Premises	3,500		
Others	2,500	6,000	18,900
Net Profit			93,600

Balance Sheet

	Cost (€)	Depreciation (€)	Net (€)
Fixed Assets			
Premises	70,000	3,500	66,500
Others	50,000	2,500	47,500
	120,000	6,000	114,000
Less Current Assets			
Stock	7,000		
Debtors (2 Months' Sales)	77,500		
Bank	22,950		
		107,450	
Less Current Liabilities			
Creditors (1 × Purchases)	16,000		
Expenses	850	16,850	90,600
			204,600
Financed by			
Capital	120,000		
Plus Net Profit	93,600		
	213,600		
Less Drawings	9,000		
			€204,600

Question 14.5

Barnacarroll Plc requires you to prepare a month-by-month cash budget for the second half of 2010 based on the following information.

1. The company's only product sells at €60. It has a variable cost of €39, made up as follows: labour €6, material €30, overheads €3.
2. Fixed costs of €9,000 per month are paid on the last day of each month.
3. Credit sales quantities are as follows.

May	June	July	Aug	Sept	Oct	Nov	Dec
1,500	1,800	2,100	2,400	2,700	3,000	3,300	3,900

4. Production quantities are as follows.

May	June	July	Aug	Sept	Oct	Nov	Dec
1,800	2,100	2,400	3,000	3,600	3,900	3,300	

5. Credit customers are to be given two months' credit.
6. Cash sales at a discount of five per cent are expected to average 200 units per month.
7. Suppliers of raw material give one month's credit.
8. Wages are paid in the month they are incurred.
9. The variable overhead is paid in the month following production.

Solution to Question 14.5

Credit Sales = Instruction 3 × €60 moved forward two months
Cash Sales = 200 × €60 − 5%

Barnacarroll Plc Sales Budget Receipts

	July (€'000)	Aug (€'000)	Sept (€'000)	Oct (€'000)	Nov (€'000)	Dec (€'000)
Credit	90	108	126	144	162	180
Cash	11.4	11.4	11.4	11.4	11.4	11.4
Total I	101.4	119.4	137.4	155.4	173.4	191.4

Material = No. 4 × 730 plus one month
Wages = No. 4 × 76
Overhead = No. 4 × 73 plus one month

Payments

	July (€)	Aug (€)	Sept (€)	Oct (€)	Nov (€)	Dec (€)
Material	63	72	90	108	117	108
Wages	14.4	18	21.6	23.4	21.6	19.8
Overheads	6.3	7.2	9	10.8	11.7	10.8
Fixed	9	9	9	9	9	9
Total II	92.7	106.2	129.6	151.2	159.3	147.6
Net Cash I–II	8.7	13.2	7.8	3.2	14.1	43.8

Question 14.6

Planxty Ltd manufacture a single product. Flexible budgets have been prepared below for activity levels of 70 per cent and 100 per cent:

Flexible Budgets

Activity Level Units	70% 7,000 €	100% 10,000 €
Direct Materials	42,000	60,000
Direct Labour	21,000	30,000
Production Overheads	31,000	37,000
Administration Overheads	28,000	28,000
Distribution Overheads	20,500	25,000
Total	142,500	180,000

Profit is 25 per cent of selling price.

(a) Management has decided that a budget of 90 per cent is required and that this should then be restated using marginal costing.

or

(b) The actual results were:

Sales (8,000 units)	190,000
Materials	46,000
Labour	25,000
Production overheads	32,000
Administration overheads	27,000
Distribution overheads	22,000

Compare the budget with the actual.

Solution to Question 14.6

(i) Production Overheads

	€	Units
High	37,000	10,000
Low	31,000	7,000
	6,000	3,000

The variable element is €2 per unit @ 10,000 = €20,000 variable, total = €37,000 and fixed = €17,000.

(ii) Distribution Overheads

	€	Units
High	25,000	10,000
Low	20,500	7,000
	4,500	3,000

The variable element is €1.50 per unit @ 10,000 units = 15,000 variable, total = €25,000 and fixed €10,000.

(iii) Flexible Budget @ 90 per cent

		€
Direct Material	(9,000 × €6)	54,000
Direct Labour	(9,000 × €3)	27,000
Production Overheads	(9,000 × €2) + €17,000	35,000
Administration Overheads		28,000
Distribution Overheads	(9,000 × €1.50) + €10,000	23,500
Total		167,500
Profit		58,333
Sales		225,833

(iv) Marginal Costing

Sales		225,833
Less Variable Costs		
Materials	54,000	
Labour	27,000	
Production Overheads	18,000	
Distribution Overheads	13,500	112,500

Contribution		113,333	
Fixed Costs			
Production Overheads	17,000		
Administration Overheads	28,000		
Distribution Overheads	10,000	55,000	
Profit		58,333	

or (b)

	80%	Actual	Variance
Direct Material	48,000	46,000	2,000 F
Direct Labour	24,000	25,000	(1,000) A
Production Overheads	33,000	32,000	1,000 F
Administration Overheads	28,000	27,000	1,000 F
Distribution Overheads	22,000	22,000	–
Total	155,000	152,000	3,000 F
Profit	51,667	38,000	(13,667) A
Sales	206,667	190,000	(16,667) A

15 Farm Accounts

- To be able to prepare **fully analysed** farm accounts from given information.
- To be able to give **useful advice** based on these accounts.

Agriculture is vital to our economy. Farming nowadays is a very **complex** business, subject to much outside **regulation** and rapid **change**. Information is vital to the farmer in arriving at decisions.

1. Analyse as fully as possible each enterprise within the farm.
2. Do this using separate accounts or columnar accounts.
3. Allocate as many of the expenses as you can.
4. Other items may be unallocated or allocated, e.g. evenly – but explain what you are doing.
5. Dealing with drawings and capital introduced will be the same as in incomplete records.

Farm accounts should be prepared in such a way as to give **maximum information**.

In valuing stocks, remember SSAP 9, and value at the lower of cost and net realisable value.

Question 15.1

The following is the trial balance of the Duggan family of Meadowbrook Farm who keep a complete set of double-entry accounts.

Trial Balance at 31 December 2010

	Debit (€)	Credit (€)
Stocks (1 January 2010)		
Livestock	80,000	
Feedstuffs	4,500	
Fertilisers	8,800	
Grain	21,600	
Purchases		
Livestock	38,000	
Feedstuffs	12,600	

Seeds	4,000	
Fertilisers	11,600	
Milk Receipts		78,000
Sale of Livestock		62,000
Sale of Grain		58,000
Annual Grants		26,000
Electricity	3,800	
Subcontractors	8,800	
Repairs	3,600	
Veterinary Fees	1,960	
Wages	13,500	
Insurance	2,300	
Bank	1,700	
9% Farm Development Loan		60,000
Drawings	9,810	
Capital		270,570
Farm Land and Buildings (Cost)	320,000	
Accumulated Depreciation		
Land and Buildings		10,000
Farm Machinery	42,000	
Accumulated Depreciation		
Farm Machinery		24,000
	588,570	588,570

The following information is also available:

1. Closing stocks

	Cost (€)	Market Value (€)
Livestock	65,000	95,000
Grain	22,500	17,000
Feedstuffs	3,600	3,600
Fertilisers	7,600	7,400

2. Provide for a year's loan interest.
3. Provide depreciation at the rate of 20 per cent of cost per annum on farm machinery and one per cent of cost per annum on farm buildings (cost €120,000). Land is not depreciated.

4. Value of farm produce used by family is €4,000.
5. Allocate the following:

	Livestock and Milk (%)	Grain (%)
Wages	70	30
Subcontractors	40	60
Repairs	60	40
Others	50	50

6. Electricity due is €400.

Prepare in as much detail as possible:

(a) The enterprise and final accounts.
(b) The balance sheet.

Solution to Question 15.1

(a) Duggan Family/Meadowbrook Farm Enterprise Analysis Accounts
for the Year Ended 31 December 2010

	Milk and Cattle (€)	Grain (€)
Sales (78,000 + 62,000)	140,000	58,000
Annual Grant	13,000	13,000
	153,000	71,000
Less Costs		
Opening Stock	80,000	21,600
Purchases	38,000	4,000
	118,000	25,600
Less Closing Stock	65,000	17,000
Cost	53,000	8,600
Electricity	2,100	2,100
Subcontractors	3,520	5,280
Repairs	2,160	1,440
Veterinary Fees	1,960	
Wages	9,450	4,050
Insurance	1,150	1,150
Loan Interest	2,700	2,700
Depreciation		
Machinery	4,200	4,200
Farm Buildings	600	600
Fertiliser	6,500	6,500
Feedstuffs	13,500	
	100,840	36,620
Profit	52,160	34,380

Note: All expenses have been allocated.

Farm Profit and Loss

	(€)
Profit on Milk and Livestock	52,160
Profit on Grain	34,380
Produce Used by Family	4,000
Total to Balance Sheet	90,540

(b) Balance Sheet at 31 December 2010

	Cost (€)	Accumulated Depreciation (€)	Net Value (€)
Fixed Assets			
Land and Buildings	320,000	11,200	308,800
Machinery	42,000	32,400	9,600
	362,000	43,600	318,400
Current Assets			
Stocks: Livestock	65,000		
Grain	17,000		
Feedstuffs	3,600		
Fertilisers	7,400	93,000	
Bank		1,700	
		94,700	
Current Liabilities			
Loan Interest	5,400		
Electricity	400	5,800	
Net Current Assets			88,900
			407,300
Financed by			
Capital	270,570		
Plus Net Profit	90,540		
	361,110		
Less Drawings	13,810	347,300	
9% Farm Loan		60,000	
			€407,300

Question 15.2

Jimmy Tolan farms a mixed farming enterprise. He does not keep a full set of accounts and provides you with the following information for the year 2010:

He had the following assets and liabilities at 1 January 2010: land and buildings €230,000; machinery €35,000; stock of cattle €60,000; stock of sheep €40,000; stock of feedstuffs €3,600; electricity due €560; insurance prepaid €450 (three months); bank €6,800.

Note: All farm receipts are lodged and all payments are made by cheque.

His bank statements for the year reveal the following:

Lodgements: sale of cattle €110,000; sale of sheep €40,000; headage and premium receipts €43,000.

Payments: cattle €40,000; sheep €60,000; electricity €1,500; diesel €1,800; insurance (12 months) €2,000; silage and haymaking €16,300; fertilisers €4,600; drawings €15,000; veterinary fees €1,650; casual labour €2,400; interest €4,000; loan instalment €10,000.

On 1 July 2010 he borrowed €100,000, which was used to purchase some adjoining land. The rate of interest was to be 12 per cent payable monthly in arrears. The loan was to be repaid in 10 equal instalments on 31 December each year.

One-quarter of the following are to be regarded as drawings: insurance paid, electricity used and diesel paid.

On 31 December he had the following assets and liabilities: stock of cattle €70,000; stock of sheep €50,000; fertiliser €1,000; feedstuffs €5,400; electricity bill due €480.

Prepare:

The final accounts for the year ended 31 December 2010 and a balance sheet at the same date.

Solution to Question 15.2

Jimmy Tolan, Farmer Capital

	Debit (€)	Credit (€)
1 January		
Land and Buildings	230,000	
Machinery	35,000	
Stock		
Cattle	60,000	
Sheep	40,000	
Feed	3,600	
Electricity Due		560
Insurance Prepaid	450	
Bank	6,800	
Capital		375,290
	375,850	375,850

Profit and Loss Account for Year Ended 31 December 2010

Sales			
Cattle		110,000	
Sheep		40,000	
Headage and Premium		43,000	193,000
Less Expenses			
Cattle Opening Stock	60,000		
Add Purchases	40,000		
	100,000		
Less Closing Stock	70,000	30,000	
Sheep Opening Stock	40,000		
Add Purchases	60,000		
	100,000		
Less Closing Stock	50,000	50,000	
OR if these are allocated show the following.			
Gross Profit: Cattle		80,000	
Gross Loss: Sheep		(10,000)	
Headage, etc.		43,000	
(but part of the headage would be for sheep)			113,000
Feedstuffs (1 January)	3,600		
For Silage and Haymaking	16,300		
	19,900		
Less Feedstuffs (31 December)	5,400	14,500	
Fertiliser	4,600		
Less Stock (31 December)	1,000	3,600	
Veterinary Fees		1,650	
Casual Labour		2,400	
Interest		6,000	
Electricity		1,065	
Insurance		1,450	
Diesel		1,350	
			32,015
Net Profit			80,985

Electricity Account

	(€)		(€)
Bank	1,500	Balance	560
Balance	480	Drawings	355
		Profit and Loss	1,065
	1,980		1,980

Insurance Account

	(€)		(€)
Balance	450	Drawings	500
Bank	2,000	Profit and Loss	1,450
		Balance	500
	2,450		2,450

Diesel Account

	(€)		(€)
Bank	1,800	Drawings	450
		Profit and Loss	1,350
	1,800		1,800

Balance Sheet at 31 December 2010

	(€)	(€)	(€)
Fixed Assets			
Land and Buildings			330,000
Machinery			35,000
			365,000
Current Assets			
Stock: Cattle	70,000		
Sheep	50,000		
Fertiliser	1,000		
Feedstuffs	5,400		
Insurance Prepaid	500		
Bank	40,550		
		167,450	
Current Liabilities			
ESB Bill	480		
Interest	2,000		
	2,480	2,480	
Working Capital			164,970
			529,970
Financed by			
Capital		375,290	
Add Net Profit		80,985	
Less Drawings		(16,305)	439,970
Loan			90,000
			€529,970

Question 15.3

The following is the trial balance of a farmer, James Keogh, who keeps a complete set of double-entry accounts:

Trial Balance at 31 December 2010

	(€)	(€)
Farm Land and Buildings	250,000	
Farm Machinery at Cost	27,000	
Accumulative Depreciation – Farm Machinery		15,000
Stocks 1 January		
Livestock	70,000	
Grain	18,500	
Fertilisers	9,400	
Purchases		
Livestock	24,700	
Feeding Stuffs	7,600	
Seeds	3,900	
Fertilisers	21,250	
Sale of Grain		10,000
Sale of Cattle		39,300
Receipts from Creamery for Milk		27,750
Farm Wages	8,500	
Diesel Oil and Petrol	4,900	
Electricity	1,260	
Rates	3,440	
Repairs to Farm Machinery	725	
Veterinary Fees and Medicines	1,275	
Subcontractors for Harvesting	2,700	
Drawings	5,800	
Creditors for Fertilisers		3,900
Bank Overdraft		7,500
Bank Interest	1,300	
Capital		313,800
Loan from Agricultural Corporation		50,000
Loan Interest	5,000	
	467,250	467,250

The following additional information is available.

1. Closing stocks:

	Cost (€)	Market Value (€)
Grain	30,000	40,000
Fertilisers	9,750	12,000
Cattle	120,000	125,000

2. Value of farm produce used by Keogh and family is €2,600.
3. Depreciation of farm machinery is computed at 10 per cent of cost.
4. The December cheque from the creamery amounting to €1,850 was not received until 20 January.
5. The amount of €4,000 is due to subcontractors for harvest work, and one-quarter of the rates has been paid in advance.
6. Farm wages and fertilisers should be allocated as one-half to cattle and milk and one-half to crops.
7. On 31 December, €5,000 due for rent from Conacre had not yet been received.

Prepare:

(a) Enterprise analysis accounts.

(b) Final accounts and balance sheet at 31 December 2010.

(c) Advise James Keogh on whether his two major enterprises should be continued.

Solution to Question 15.3

(a) Enterprise Analysis Account of Cattle and Milk for the Year Ended 31 December 2010

	(€)		(€)
Opening Stock – Cattle	70,000	Sale of Cattle	39,300
Purchases	24,700	Sale of Milk	29,600
Feedstuffs	7,600	Closing Stock – Cattle	120,000
Wages	4,250		
Veterinary Fees	1,275		
Fertilisers	10,450		
Gross Profit Transferred to Trading Account	70,625		
	188,900		188,900

Enterprise Analysis Account of Crops for the Year Ended 31 December 2010

	(€)		(€)
Opening Stock – Grain	18,500	Sale of Grain	10,000
Purchase of Seeds	3,900	Closing Stock of Grain	30,000
Fertilisers	10,450	Transferred to Trading	3,800
Wages	4,250		
Subcontractor for Harvesting	6,700		
	43,800		43,800

(b) Trading Account for the Year Ended 31 December 2010

	(€)
Gross Profit on Cattle and Milk	70,625
Add Produce Used by Family	2,600
	73,225
Less Loss on Crops	3,800
Gross Profit Transferred to Profit and Loss Account	69,425

Profit and Loss Account for the Year Ended 31 December 2010

	(€)	(€)
Gross Profit from Trading Account		69,425
Add Rent Due from Conacre		5,000
Less Expenses		
Diesel Oil and Petrol	4,900	
Electricity	1,260	
Rates	2,580	
Repairs to Farm Machinery	725	
Bank Interest	1,300	
Loan Interest	5,000	
Depreciation on Machinery	2,700	18,465
Net Profit		55,960

Balance Sheet at 31 December 2006

	Cost (€)	Accumulated Depreciation (€)	Book Value (€)
Fixed Assets			
Land and Buildings	250,000		250,000
Machinery	27,000	17,700	9,300
	277,000	17,700	259,300
Current Assets			
Stocks: Grain	30,000		
Cattle	120,000		
Fertilisers	9,750	159,750	
Debtor (Creamery)		1,850	
Rent Received Due		5,000	
Rates Prepaid		860	
		167,460	
Less Current Liabilities			
Creditors – Fertilisers	3,900		
Subcontractors	4,000		
Bank Overdraft	7,500	15,400	152,060
			411,360
Financed by			
Capital			313,800
Add Net Profit			55,960
			369,760
Less Drawings			8,400
			361,360
Long-Term Liabilities			
Loan from Agricultural Corporation			50,000
			411,360

(c)
He is losing money on his crops enterprise and this may be discontinued, although farm enterprises which make a loss in one year may be profitable in another.

aims
- To know the four fundamental accounting concepts.
- To know how the accountancy profession is regulated and the duties of the different people involved.

Concepts you must know

SSAP 2

SSAP 2 recognises four fundamental accounting concepts:

> **key point**
>
> SSAPs stands for Statements of Standard Accounting Practice.

1. Going concern
2. Consistency
3. Accruals
4. Prudence.

1. Going concern

The accounts are prepared on the assumption that the business will continue into the future.

2. Consistency

Accounting items will be treated in the same way from one period to the next, e.g. depreciation of 20 per cent of cost will not be changed overnight to 30 per cent written-down value.

3. Accruals

'Accruals' is also a matching concept. Expenses for a period should be allocated to that period. Expenses for a period paid or unpaid must be included. Expenses prepaid will be excluded.

4. Prudence

'Prudence' is also known as the concept of conservatism. This says that losses should always be anticipated, but not gains. Only realised gains should be taken into account. Always refer back to this concept.

SSAP 9: Stock

Stock is valued at the lower of cost and net realisable value. This is simply the concept of prudence restated. If stock goes down in value, it is the lower figure that should be used; but if it goes up in value, it should not be valued at the higher figure.

How accounting is regulated

Companies are obliged to prepare an annual **profit and loss account** and **balance sheet**. Large and medium companies are obliged to also publish a **cash flow statement**. Companies must also present an **annual report** to the shareholders at the **Annual General Meeting**. This report will include:

- The directors' report
- The auditors' report
- The financial statements.

Regulatory bodies

There are four regulatory bodies:

1. The government
2. The accountancy profession
3. The stock exchange
4. The European Union.

Government regulation

Under the 1963 Companies Act, directors are responsible for preparing and presenting the accounts in proper format.

Under the 1986 Companies Act, which is an extension of the 1963 Act, the Fourth Directive of the EU was enacted. It sets out the format for presentation of the accounts. The Act classifies three types of companies – small, medium and large. It sets out three criteria for classification, all three of which must be attained.

Classification of small and medium companies

Criteria	Small	Medium
Turnover	<€3m	>€3m and <€12m
Total of balance sheet	<€1.5m	>€1.5m and <€6m
Employees	<50	>50 and <250

Note: All other companies are large.

Full disclosure must be made by all public companies and large private companies. However, medium and small private companies do not need to disclose as much information. Information must be disclosed to the shareholders and the registrar of companies – that is, it must be **filed**.

Disclosure requirements of companies

Leabharlanna Fhine Gall

	Public and Large Private		Medium Private		Small Private	
	Members	Filed	Members	Filed	Members	Filed
Profit and Loss	Full	Full	Short	Short	Short	None
Balance Sheet	Full	Full	Full	Abridged	Abridged	Abridged

Note: All must give a true and fair view.

Regulation by the accountancy profession

The accountancy profession have made the preparation of accounts more consistent. This has been achieved by issuing **Statements of Standard Accounting Practice** (SSAPs) and **Financial Reporting Standards** (FRSs). This standardisation makes it easier to compare between companies and from year to year.

Regulation by the stock exchange

Companies that are quoted on the stock exchange are required to make extra **disclosures**. This is for the benefit of shareholders and the general public. Among these are:

1. Half yearly accounts
2. Geographical breakdown of turnover and profits
3. A statement giving the interest of each director in the share capital.

Regulation by the European Union

The EU issues **directives** that aim to standardise or harmonise accounting practice within the member states. This is done by issuing directives.

Among the directives issued have been those on the format of profit and loss accounts and balance sheets of companies and group companies. The eighth directive governed the qualification and regulation of auditors.

The auditors

The auditors are independent accountants who are appointed by the shareholders and can only be removed by shareholders.

All auditors are accountants but not all accountants are auditors.

It is the directors, not the auditors, who have to prepare the accounts. The **auditors' job** is to report on the preparation of the accounts by the directors to the shareholders in standard format annually.

Their report will be 'unqualified' or 'qualified'. An **unqualified** report tells the shareholders that the auditors have found that the accounts are accurate. If the auditors are not satisfied, they must state this in the form of a **qualified** report.

If the auditors discover **fraud**, they must report it, although detecting fraud is not their primary function. The audit should be conducted with due care and diligence.